CW00548445

ANOTHER TEAR FALLS

A Study Of Scott Walker

◆

Jeremy Reed

credits

another tear falls
an appreciation of scott walker
by:
jeremy reed
ISBN 1 871592 75 5
© jeremy reed 1998
first published 1998 by:
creation books
london • san francisco
this edition © creation books 1998
design/layout/typesetting:
pcp international, bradley davis
design technician:
extra-sensory design
photo credits:
photographs by courtesy of antar archives

author's acknowledgements

thank you to the inspirers: this book grew out of my conversations with john robinson about scott, and I thank him for listening to the book as it progressed, and for his constant encouragement. I also thank john balance and peter christopherson, for being there for me, and my publisher, james williamson, for enthusiastic support.

the author would like to thank owen michael brown for his generosity in typing this manuscript.

—*J.R.*

This book is for
Lene Rasmussen

CONTENTS

ANOTHER TEAR FALLS

"For you and me it's better to be unknown – to do our work."
—John Wieners, 707 Scott Street

"Night is thy Hearse, whose sable Canopie
Covers alike deceased day and thee.
And all those weeping dewes which nightly fall,
Are but the tears shed for thy funerall."
—Henry King (1592–1669)

"Anyway, they're a waste of time, regrets."
—Scott Walker

"We poets in our youth begin in gladness
But thereof come in the end despondency and madness."
—William Wordsworth

BLANKET ROLL BLUES

There's always two of Scott. The one we think he is – Scott Walker – and the other one who he really is: Noel Scott Engel. It's a psychological dichotomy that runs throughout the man's career. The name, Scott Walker, conjures to mind the dramatic baritone balladeer, pitching his indigo-mood octaves above a Wagnerian wall of orchestral sound. Scott's manner of singing finds its analogue in a surfer climbing the roller's high peak, and staying there in the dazzled run for shore that occupies a recording time of 3:31.

But Noel Scott Engel. Who is the reclusively introspective individual, who has chosen to keep his private life an almost inviolable secret? We know little more about his ordinariness than we do of the enigmatic life and death of Isidore Ducasse, the self-styled Comte de Lautréamont, author of *Les Chants de Maldoror*. Ducasse, who adopted the pseudonym Lautréamont, in the way Engel elected the persona Walker, died – most probably by his own hand – on 24 November, 1870, in a modest hotel, 7 Faubourg-Montmartre. He was twenty-four years old, and his poetic legacy *Maldoror* has proved to be one of the most subversively influential of texts to succeeding generations of literary iconoclasts. It's quite possible that Lautréamont's visions terrified Ducasse, in the way that Walker's initial success threatened Engel.

Lautréamont was correct in what he said of Ducasse: "I shall leave no memoirs." Walker has implied the same for Engel, and the apparent discontinuity of dialogue between man and artist has resulted in an increasing creative silence, broken only once in the last fifteen years by the release of *Tilt* in 1995.

One could argue that *Maldoror* was written for posthumous acclaim. But the gradient of Scott Walker's career in music is one that has been subject to the variants of success, obscurity and re-discovery. Singers, like writers, often undergo a virtual death before being reassessed by a later generation. There was a time stretching from the late-sixties up until the 1981 compilation, *Fire Escape In The Sky: The God-Like Genius Of Scott Walker*, when Scott solo albums were unobtainable other than through second-hand purchases. The Walker voice had temporarily gone on hold in the underworld. But the legend of a tormented singer, all high cheekbones and aesthetic features partly obscured by dark shades and a forbidding blond fringe had persisted as an indelible image in the pop psyche.

Over the years we have often come to mistake a new Scott Walker recording for a posthumous release. What for instance induced Walker to break a decade's silence in 1993 to record the enigmatic single, "Man From Reno/Indecent Sacrifice", as part of the soundtrack for a French-language film called *Toxic Affair*? And why subsequent to the critical approbation attendant on *Tilt*, should Walker agree to record an insignificant Bob Dylan composition, "I Threw It All Away", as part of the soundtrack for *To Have And To Hold*? The apparent illogistics behind such creative decisions are as clandestine as Scott himself.

The Scott Walker myth feeds on the notion of eternal return: the young man who has never really gone away. CD re-issues have Scott freeze-framed in time, his face as it was thirty years ago, unalterably isolated within the frozen precincts of a photograph. It's within the romantic context of the artwork for *Scott, Scott 2, Scott 3*, and *Scott 4*, that we locate the image that accompanies the voice. The moodily disillusioned torch-singer portrayed on the CD inlays is the persisting idea of Scott Walker, no matter how much his person and music have changed over the decades. Record sleeves have come to invest their subjects with the illusion of immutable youth. We buy into an artist photographed in 1970, and suspend our belief that he or she has been altered by time. The concept of endowing singers with permanent youth is one of the record industry's most successful deceptions.

In terms of image then, Scott Walker is constantly misassessed by his record buying public. The older Scott, who agreed to be photographed for interviews accompanying the release of *Tilt*, is facially unchanged, although the hair is shorter, and the absorption of experiential pain, more clearly written into the features. The *Tilt*-Scott is streamlined to meet with the apocalyptic nihil evoked by his most recent music. He looks distinctly modern without any least attempt to do so. The shades have persisted as part of the necessary process of screening out reality, and they are prominent as a visual link with his past. And so too is the pervading sense of integrity that the man manifests in speaking of his art. In Scott's terms, there is no other direction than that of truth. If a commercial sacrifice is made, then it's in the interests of artistic expression.

One of the reasons Scott gives to account for his eleven years silence between *Climate Of Hunter* and *Tilt*, is his apprehension that record companies would show little or no interest in the genre of music he was creating. In an interview with Simon Williams, published in the *NME*, 20 May 1995, he will say: "I wouldn't write because there was this thing whereby you had to make demos, and I can't imagine demoing any of my material. The idea is totally ridiculous. So I didn't enter that game and because nobody could hear anything, nobody seemed to be interested. So I simply took years off."

This disarmingly casual defence of his creative inertia, is of course only an aspect of the problem. In the single interview he gave Richard Cook for 1984's *Climate Of Hunter* album, Scott was not only affirmative about his new suite of songs, but also confident of a new, regenerative momentum. He claimed his voice had become a more resonant instrument with age. "This is the best age to sing at – until you reach 50, when it starts to go down," he commented. "Right now, you're at your peak. I was very worried about it, but once I started it was easier than I've ever found before."

Interviewed by the same Richard Cook, eleven years on, in May 1995, for *The Wire*, Scott will present his notion of singing in different terms. "Singing's always hard for me," he asserted. "Not physically. But to get it neutral, where it's not too emotional and not too deadpan. Somewhere in between is what I'm looking for. It drives me crazy sometimes. In this case, I think it's a little better than some of the shots I've had at it."

In the same interview, Scott will elaborate on his working method in the studio. "I usually sing afterwards," he volunteered, "so the musicians don't know what's going on. But I don't do a lot of takes and I don't rehearse it at home. So I'm surprised as well, when I'm doing the vocal. I have the spontaneity. I don't always sing what I've written, but I might keep it anyway. In the 'Bouncer' song I didn't sing a line as it was written, but because I felt I couldn't improve on the take, I kept it."

Both *Climate Of Hunter* and *Tilt* approximate to neutral tones of singing, but the desired effect is also achieved through partial loss of perfect diction. The impeccable diction that characterises Scott's ballad singing throughout the sixties and seventies is sacrificed as the voice works to complement the music by becoming part of the instrumentation. Scott's later vocals, oscillating between baritone and tenor are also pitched to accommodate non-linear lyrics. The mosaic of splinter-line allusions that comprises the lyric texture of *Climate Of Hunter*, is by its hermetic content unsuited to the linear-narrative mode of singing that distinguishes Scott's earlier work. And in fact on *Tilt,* where the voice is mixed further back than on any other Walker album, Scott's phrasing attracts not so much by emphasising individual words, but by attending to a group of words, as though it is the disquieting subtext to neutral tone. When the operatic baritone is unleashed on "Patriot (A Single)", the power blows the listener away. Scott's voice is almost unconfrontable in a listening space, as he allows us two twenty-second reminders of a baritone pitch that lifts subterranean hurt from the soul into breath. It's as if all the years of silence are being redeemed by these two dramatic choruses.

Speaking at the time of *Tilt*'s release of the blank interludes of his career, and of the self-loathing that had him resort to alcohol, Scott turned the issue on a moral axis, questioning: "Do I feel as though I did anything wrong? No, not through those times. I might have done earlier on, but I can't remember what they were because I was pretty gone. I can't remember anything. Anyway, they're a waste of time, regrets."

Scott's inveterate guardedness within the interview arena is the justifiable prerogative of any artist who wishes to make a distinction between his private and public lives. What the man does over the days, months, years and decades surfaces obliquely within the context of the voice, and the synthesis of experience gained is crystallised in the making of a new record. Scott's inner journey as he experienced it through the eighties and the early part of the nineties is evident on *Tilt,* no matter how esoteric are the references provided.

Ever since the massive hits scored by the Walker Brothers in the mid-sixties, Scott Walker has set about deconstructing the image of himself as a commercially successful pop star. The tear-jerker Bacharach/David ballads to which Scott leant a vocal prowess rarely encountered before in pop, relied for their impact not only on the threesome's good looks, but also on the Phil Spector-like wall of orchestral sound afforded the songs by Ivor Raymonde. But for all the rotund baritone architecture applied to hits like "Make It Easy On Yourself", "The Sun Ain't Gonna Shine Anymore", and "My Ship Is Coming In", the songs proved to be dramatic exceptions to the predominant R&B, and drum, bass, and two guitar bands who dominated the upper echelons of the charts. Not that there wasn't a place for crooners and balladeers. Roy Orbison, Elvis Presley, Gene Pitney and Billy Fury on the male front, had all provided voices for a soft-focused, bluely down-mooded boy meets girl ballad, in which the inevitable outcome is heartbreak or unrequited love. It wasn't that the Walker Brothers embraced profounder themes; the real difference lay in Scott's approaching the song with a torch-singer's extravagant do-or-die conviction. Because Scott appeared to identify with the lyrics he was singing, so his audience early on came to associate him with the solitary mood evoked by many of the songs. Lines like "Loneliness is a cloak you wear/A deep shade of blue is always there" seemed to fit directly with the genuinely anguished singer. Hidden behind dark shades, and far too intellectually serious for his iconization as a teen idol, Scott was every bit the wounded romantic that his image suggested.

Scott, who palpably recoiled from his teenage fan-base was only too aware of the short-lived nature of stardom, and of the likelihood that he was being idolized more for his looks, than his voice. With most Walker Brothers' concerts degenerating into a debacle of hysterical fans, rendering Scott's voice inaudible, there seemed little place for Walker's aspirations to deliver serious, literate songs. Awkward on stage, in contrast to John Maus's extrovert movements, Scott had right from the start appeared painfully self-conscious, and radically disconnected from the audience to whom he was singing. If Scott's paranoid disposition had already been triggered by the unnatural pressures that stardom involves, so too one sensed a shade of embarrassment on his part at using such a voice within the pop milieu. The rich, pain-sensitive timbre of Scott's voice marked him as an outsider from the start. Black shades enhanced the aura of mystery surrounding the singer, and interviewed in 1967, Scott gave authenticity to his by now legendary solitude. "I live the life of a recluse," he commented, "not out of choice or any mistaken notion that I am creating an image or sympathy for myself, but because this is the way I am."

The legend of the existentially alienated singer living constantly on the cutting edge was enforced by Scott's apparent suicide attempt on August 15 1966. Walker, who was taken from his gas-filled flat at Dudley Court, near Regent's Park, to St. Mary's Hospital, Paddington, received treatment before being released the following day. According to Scott aficionados, this reported incident of attempted suicide was the first of numerous attempts by the singer over the years to terminate his existence. It was also a serious move on Scott's part to dismantle his celebrity status, and to begin the inner journey towards individual freedom of artistic expression, which has culminated in the almost anonymous individual who cut *Tilt*. The artist who has appeared briefly for interviews related to *Climate Of Hunter*, and *Tilt*, is someone disencumbered of the protocol attached to pop status, and therefore free to express himself in the interests of artistic conviction. Scott's air-sealed privacy is now accepted as the psychological precinct in which he lives and creates. There's a distinct possibility that at the moment I'm writing this essay on a cloud-roofed London afternoon, Scott concealed behind his familiar shades, and dressed in a green anorak and blue jeans, is out cycling on the road between Bayswater and Chiswick. There's no great mystery behind somebody exercising on a bike, but because the figure is Scott Walker, this ordinary habit is almost the beginnings of a fiction.

What Scott has learnt is that he can never escape the fingerprint left by his voice. Making a record is like writing a book. The thing will never quite go away. Scott claims to keep no copies of his past recordings, and to have dissociated himself from his former role as a torch-singer. But the songs exist independent of him, as an eponymous reminder to the listener that the recorded voice lives in a state of disembodied timelessness, as the word also adopts an autonomous life of its own on the page. CD cases resemble rectangular coffins, the music inside awaiting resurrection on disc.

In the early part of the eighties, when the Scott Walker legend had been buried deep underground, his reputation was in part re-activated by obsessional enthusiasts like Julian Cope, and Marc Almond. Cope was untiring in his propagation of Walker as a neglected genius, and Marc Almond was to include a version of Scott's "Big Louise", on his 1981 *Untitled* album, and to use another Scott composition, "The Plague", as part of his live repertoire. Almond, who was as the decade evolved to become Britain's premier torch-singer, is arguably the only successor to Walker's torch legacy. Similarly influenced by the Belgian singer/songwriter, Jacques Brel, and like Scott willing to work assiduously with a voice-coach, Almond's tenor range, with its baroque flourishes, grew in stature to become in its genre, an instrument as unique as Scott's. Almond was quick to adapt songs like "In My Room", and "If You Go Away" – both Scott successes – to his own method of phrasing; but was anxious not to be construed as a surrogate for the absent maestro. It says much for Scott's temerity in discovering unconventional material, that Marc Almond has been the only subsequent artist willing to risk applying his talent to songs that are considered to be indelible constituents of Walker's oeuvre.

Almond may be seen as one of the last heroic survivors of a genre of acoustic balladeers prepared to make themselves vulnerable through taking on songs in which the poetic lyrics are matched by the epic proportions of orchestrated melody. On the superb suite of cover songs, "A Woman's Story", Almond delivers an impassioned rendition of Walker's "The Plague", and approaches each of the songs covered on this mini-album with a vocal authority answerable to Scott alone. Like Walker at the time of his late sixties prolificacy, Almond is an isolated figure without contemporaries. His two albums of French covers, *Jacques* and *Absinthe*, owe their origins to Walker's early admiration for the songs of Jacques Brel and Charles Aznavour.

Almond, on *Absinthe*, has taken the process a stage further, by recording lyrics by the French poets Charles Baudelaire and Arthur Rimbaud, as well as highly controversial material in the form of Serge Lama's "The Slave", and Barbara's "Incestuous Love". Almost a quarter of a century earlier, Scott had undoubtedly shocked his listeners with the sexually explicit lyrics of his Brel covers of "Jackie" and "Next", on *Scott 2*. And like Scott, who succeeded in taking "Jackie" into the singles charts, despite the airwaves ban placed on the song, Almond resurrected "Jackie" (as "Jacky") in 1991, and drove it into the Top Twenty on the back of an extravagantly camp O.T.T. disco-beat. Both singers are amongst the most uncompromisingly brilliant of their respective generations.

The Scott Walker who recorded *Tilt*, which may in time, stand as his masterpiece, was someone disaffiliated from contemporary pop, and a person come back from the experiential abyss to report on his findings. "I didn't listen to a lot of pop when I was doing this," he will say, "because you subconsciously reference a lot. I listened to Beethoven's piano sonatas throughout and some Bartok string quartets. And some blues records. After it, I did what I used to do and gathered in every single that was going on and listened to all of it, to be sure that the recording was going to be what I wanted. I can tell you where it comes from. It comes from silence, most of it. I sit around and I'm waiting. I'm waiting and waiting."

Tilt sounds like the musical accompaniment to Samuel Beckett's progressively minimal texts published over the last two decades of the author's life. Reading the published lyrics that come with the album, I'm aware that Scott's typographic placement of words, together with their disjunctive syntax seems to look back to the innovative French poet, Pierre Reverdy, or to the experimental writings of John Cage and William Burroughs. Scott is endeavouring to have language emulate film. His allusive, kinetic images resemble non-sequential film-frames, each line haloed by an isolation that separates it from the next. There's often little run-on line meaning, and the lyric works by counterpointing incongruous images, one against the other.

Of his writing technique in relation to *Tilt*, Scott will tell us: "I'll start an idea, the next part might come up in a couple of months. Nothing's wasted at all. I'll read something or see something and think, that's where that goes... I'm trying to go for something as carved down as possible."

The lyrics on *Tilt* are even more liposuction-streamlined than those belonging to *Climate Of Hunter*. Their anatomy is anorexic, like a Giacometti sculpture. It's Scott's voice that feeds breath into their attenuated organisms.

Let's keep backtracking and fastforwarding through Scott's career. Even at the peak of the Walker Brothers' commercial popularity, Scott appeared to be working as an undercover saboteur of hit formula, and towards realigning his artistic credibility within the band. How else account for his incorporating the use of a pipe organ at the Leicester Square Odeon cinema, into the production of his self-penned "Archangel", the B-side to "Deadlier Than The Male". There's a tenuous link between the eccentric genius manifested on "Archangel", the spookily disquieting "The Electrician" from 1978's *Nite Flights*, and "Bouncer See Bouncer" from *Tilt*, on which Brian Gascoigne can be heard playing the organ of the Methodist Central Hall in Islington.

The three songs spaced almost at intervals of a decade between each other, would by themselves confirm Scott's reputation as a genius. The funereal organ apart, "Archangel" proceeds to endow an introspective lyric of waiting for angelic intervention with a sombre mysticism. The unconscious death-wish that informs most of Scott's lyric writing in the late sixties is given form in "Archangel" through the solitary narrator's sense of exclusion from reality. "Archangel", and "Mrs. Murphy", from the same period, are the prototypes for a particular outsider narrative that runs uniformly through Scott's early solo projects. "Archangel" is the blueprint for "Montague Terrace In Blue", "The Amorous Humphrey Plugg", and poignant studies in loneliness like "Big Louise", and "Rosemary". In these songs, Scott portrays a compassionate empathy for the socially excluded, and with the lonely in cities, whose inner dialogue is punctuated by a voyeuristic concern with anonymous neighbours.

In specifically writing about outsiders, Scott invented a genre of expression that had not previously found inclusion in pop music. His objective, almost dispassionately observed novellas within song, extended to "Big Louise", arguably the first lyric to be devoted to a transsexual. In Scott's portrayal of his subject, Louise is the victim of conspiratorial neighbours who are unwilling to accept her sex-change. Scott's sympathetic treatment of the socio-psychological aspects of living outside conventions set him apart from most of his songwriting contemporaries. Again, it is Marc Almond who has most successfully taken up Scott's theme of celebrating the disaffiliated. Almond's 1981 hit with Soft Cell, "Bedsitter", was the first of a score of songs he was to devote to social outsiders living within a city ethos. If Marc Almond's preoccupations lie more with a gay and transgender milieu than Scott's, then he too has forwarded song within the context of poetically meaningful lyricism. Almond's "Exotica Rose", the B-side of his 1990 hit, "A Lover Spurned", narrates the story of a female impersonator with much the same set of sympathies as informs Scott's "Big Louise".

"The Electrician", Scott's extraordinary solo contribution to the regrouped Walker Brothers' 1978 *Nite Flights*, is one of the most harrowingly understated of songs in his disquieting oeuvre. We know that it attracted the interest of David Bowie and Brian Eno, and any retrospective evaluation of Bowie's late seventies work, suggests an unacknowledged indebtedness to the dissonant arrangements that Scott provided for *Nite Flights*. The mystico-S&M dilemma of the protagonist in "The Electrician", provides a song that infractions the listener's spiritual axis. Who is the weirdo "drilling thru the spiritus sanctus" in a room with the lights gone low? There's no way out for this individual, who claims, "if I jerk the handle you'll die in your dreams". The thrill here is in the anticipation of slow extinction. The song suggests a psychopath about to sever the mains of human consciousness. It's perhaps the most agonisingly portentous of Scott's studies in psychological alienation. Although *Nite Flights* disappeared without commercial impact, it was to leave behind a residue of critical approval instrumental to Scott's signing to Virgin records in 1980.

Scott's songwriting on *Nite Flights* was to prove the template for the even obscurer *Climate Of Hunter* and *Tilt*. The three albums, which comprise Scott's entire output over a seventeen year period may be viewed as a trilogy. This weird triumvirate of albums, with their postmodern lyric contents and minimally complex instrumentation comprises an innovative experiment as valid as any of the successes scored by the likes of pioneers like Philip Glass, Brian Eno, and his sometimes collaborator, David Bowie.

Scott's essential isolation in music is also a tribute to his integrity. Interested in neither fame, money, nor live performance, he has been a solitary innovator, prepared to create in the silence necessary to propounding a vision. Those who work alone, inhabit the great night, a nocturnal precinct celebrated by the visionary poets, Novalis, Lautréamont, Rimbaud, and Rilke, as the domain in which creative truth is encountered. Poets sit up at night, waiting for the new day, or the revelatory dawn in which the world will be transformed.

The night also provides a cover for those who are different, and the nocturnal aspects to many of Scott's songs suggest that he too feels more psychologically attuned after dark. Night walking, night thinking, or listening to rain at night, all convey their own sense of anticipation to the participant. At night we are more in touch with the unconscious, and with the underworld facets of psyche evoked by reflection and dreams. It's therefore little surprise that the opening track on *Tilt*, "Farmer In The City", should be rooted in Scott's preoccupation with the night. In a lyric subtitled, "Remembering Pasolini", and cryptically evoking the latter's violent homosexual murder, Scott's perfectly modulated, elegiac vocal pursues a metaphoric night journey. It's as though in the course of listening to the song we enter the night and deepen our exploration of its contents. "And I used to be a citizen", Scott sings, as though only too conscious of his years of reclusion.

It's therefore perfectly fitting that the second song on *Tilt*, "The Cockfighter", begins with the affirmation: "ITS A BEAUTIFUL NIGHT FROM HERE TO THOSE STARS". Scott's lyrics often comprise nocturnal thoughts, and the characters in his songs express their angularity to social norms by realising their unconscious potential at night. The writing on what I have chosen to call the trilogy of Scott's late albums is serious stuff in terms of its evincing all the signs of intense inner conflict. As guarded as always, Scott will say in his 1995 *Wire* interview: "I think I said to you before, I don't write until I'm ready to record. It's pointless, if I'm going to sit around in a wilderness because I can't record any songs... I threw a whole lot of songs away, as many as I could write. Which isn't a lot. Ever."

I suspect that a lot more of Scott's time goes into writing than he would ever lay claim to, and that the lack of any defined momentum in his output is the inhibitor that leads to his defensiveness. Creating within a time-frame, and with the objective of externalizing one's work is a very different process from that of having no prescribed aim for work that occurs at random. There's something too perfected about Scott's finished product to suggest that his compositions are the sporadic result of an unpractised spontaneity. Recent interviewers have neglected to ask him about his current interests in literature. We know only that in the sixties, and of his own admission, he read the then popular French existentialists, Sartre and Camus, and the novels of Jean Genet and Dostoyevsky. Scott's inner geography has always been sensitised by the books, films, art and music on which he picks up. He may or may not know of the quirky speed-poetry of the English experimentalist, Tom Raworth, but there are similarities between Raworth's elliptical, filmic technique, and the method of Scott's film-framed lyrics on *Tilt*.

Scott's dilemma, and one shared by all artists excluded from the mainstream is how to reach a sizeable audience without compromising artistic integrity. The cult artist always feels cheated of response, for the seriousness of the work is rarely matched by a corresponding commercial success. It is this crisis which predominantly triggers artistic suicide. Too often a work generated by subjective excitement appears to the disappointment of its creator to be defused by objective criticism. Scott would presumably like a new appreciative audience to complement his nucleus of die-hard fans. "I've no idea where this record belongs," he will say of *Tilt*, "I'm not making records for that reason... My only thing is I want to make the records. That's where I get off... But there's all kinds of artists who have different audiences for their work. I know I'm not in the mainstream at all. I'm a marginal artist. But these days so is Lou Reed or John Cale or anyone like that. I don't think I'm unusual in that kind of way."

Scott has reacted extremely over the years to the critical hype that he was poised in the late sixties to become the new Sinatra. Sinatra's idiosyncratic way of converting each of his songs into *bel canto* is a style very different from Scott's dramatically variable reading of material within Sinatra's fluent tenor range. Scott's dispositional angularity to using song as a form of entertainment, has eliminated him from a field in which Sinatra, Tony Bennett and Jack Jones have been willing to accommodate their vocal finesse to the cabaret circuit. Of these three singers, Scott appears to have learnt more from Jack Jones' phrasing, and from the arrangements to his songs, than from the illustriously consummate Sinatra and Bennett. Scott's ballad singing, nowhere better realised than on the album *Scott Sings Songs From His TV Series*, would have secured him a lucrative niche in Las Vegas. Instead, he chose to dismantle the idea of his crooning proficiency, and to react against any pre-conceived notion of the material to be encompassed by a new Scott Walker album. If one had thought of Scott's vocal spectrum as blue, then he has over the years heightened the colouring to cobalt, ultramarine, and indigo. *Tilt* is probably classifiable as black, indigo, and navy-blue.

Scott, who spent three years in the eighties on an arts course at Byam Shaw, a private college in South London, has always written to give visual conceptualisation to his songs. This is nowhere more apparent than on *Tilt*, where images of Nazi and South American concentration camps are powerfully evoked through slow-motion kinetic imagery. Always prepared to move on, Scott in dissociating himself from former achievements, will say in 1984: "I don't listen to the old songs. I don't have the records. People don't believe that, but I say you can come and listen to my apartment, like Gene Hackman."

This nomadic, almost selfless relation to his work seems also to suggest a deeply wounded individual who would rather disclaim credit for his achievements than own to criticism for their possible shortcomings. Disillusionment, in the way that Scott has clearly grown dispirited over the years by critical neglect, either generates low self-esteem in an artist or a reactionary extremism, whereby he or she cultivates hermeticism as a whiplash answer to the opposition.

It should be remembered that Scott's initial introduction to music with the inaugural Walker Brothers was on the commercial level of competing for chart domination. With their third, fourth and fifth singles releases securing No. 2, No. 3, and No. 1 places respectively in the British charts, Scott manifested signs of both welcoming and resisting his sudden icon status. Scott, who perceived with increasing perspicuity the superficiality attached to pop glamour viewed his meteoric rise to fame with nervous scepticism. Always sensitive to rejection, Scott was to reveal his ambivalent relations with success, more fully after the release of his first three solo albums, when he reacted adversely to a fractional under-reception of the work, and effectively assassinated his solo momentum through the misjudged release of *Scott 4*. Scott's paradoxical apprehension of success – he both wants it and doesn't like what it entails – seems pivotal to the inconsistencies that have marked his career.

Scott's inveterate lack of belief in himself signalled by the sort of occlusive depression that kept him from writing songs in the dormant period between 1970–78, could also be construed as a refusal to de-idealize a notion of self-perfection. Why after the Walker Brothers' reunion in 1975, and cushioned by the hit single, "No Regrets", should Scott have conceived of the idea of a projected solo album as a distinctly arduous improbability? "Now someone wants me to do a solo album of original material, and I'm really struggling hard to complete it," he offered. "It's a long haul back, man, to that dark and dark and dark... Because it's a real dark cavern."

The putative solo album of which Scott was speaking in 1977, was evidently the blueprint for the Walker Brothers' *Nite Flights*. Although John Maus and Gary Leeds are given songwriting credits on *Nite Flights*, for their individually performed contributions, it seems evident from the singularly obsessive preoccupations manifested by the lyrics that the album was universally written by Scott. Why should each of the three have chosen to employ an identical lyric style and structure in the presentation of their material? That the album would have been superior for its being a solo Scott project seems indubitable in the light of Scott's performances on "Nite Flights" and "The Electrician".

What seems to have remained constant over the years is Scott's psychological take on life. The state I have chosen to call his artistic integrity is also a way of describing Scott's awareness of a deepening rather than changing concern with ethics. Between "The Electrician", and "Rosary" from *Tilt*, which represents a time-span of almost twenty years, Scott's mental landscape seems to have remained relatively unchanged. An artist's imaginal preoccupations may not be reflected in his social relations, but they colour the depth-aspects of the individual's psyche. The real Scott is of course the occupant of his work.

Time to move on to other considerations of Scott. Another London afternoon, with rain giving the streets a glassine finish. The writer and his subject separated by the physical distance between N.W.3. and W.11. Communication is made by the empathetically charged written word. Biographies are so often an assemblage of facts without a subject. I have chosen the essay as the form in which to meet Scott.

FUNERAL TANGO

To my mind it's *Scott 3* and not the self-penned *Scott 4* which represents Walker at the summit of his first solo career. *Scott 3* combines Walker's poetic lyricism with interpretations of Jacques Brel's contentious romantic realism, and the two forces brought into sympathetic opposition unite through Scott's voice to create an eloquent masterpiece.

By contrast, I find *Scott 4* lazily undersung, deliberately self-parodying, and without the gothic elaboration legitimated by *Scott 3*. It's only a subjective nose for vintage Scott, but I feel *Scott 3* represents the ceiling of his early achievements. The Brel songs included on the album, seem in Scott's versions to add a stimulating counterpoint to his own melodic compositions. The altogether rawer and self-indulgent *Scott 4* is a record more intent on demythicizing the voice, and is in my opinion one of Scott's least successful vocal albums. The elevation of *Scott 4* to cult status during the seventies and eighties seems to have been contingent on the knowledge that the album represented at the time of its release an act of defiance on Scott's part to his record company. On its release in 1969, *Scott 4* was credited to Noel Scott Engel, the first time that the name Walker hadn't appeared on a Scott solo release. The album was a resounding commercial failure, and the blame must lie in part with the ragged manner in which Scott delivers his vocals. The impassioned authority with which the singer registers on *Scott 3* is such that he fills his material with a phrasing so sensitive that there is no overlap between the emotional subtext and the lyric sung.

Scott 4 is of course a reaction on the artist's part to having recorded three albums of similar material, the modality having been perfected in the realisation of *Scott 3*.

"*Scott 4* was all screwed up," Walker will comment in 1976. "I didn't have any management at the time. Everybody I came to thought I was a nutcase." It was a concept Scott was to revive in his *Mojo*, 1995 interview, by claiming, "A lot of people think I'm mad. Even some of the people I work with." Perhaps a more psychologically illuminating way to describe Scott's disposition is one of being alienated through the failure to compromise. Scott's lack of connection to the trivial plane on which so much commercial pop functions, and his abiding seriousness, have made it difficult over the years for him to target an audience. Both *Climate Of Hunter* and *Tilt* seem to beg the gravity of critical response we would accord a disquietingly futuristic novel. Should *Tilt* be considered a work of fiction, or is it an obliquely complex suite of neo-apocalyptic music?

Speaking in 1995 of the dissolution of the Walker Brothers as symptomatic of their being trapped in a preconceived sound, Scott will draw attention to the inhibitors that prevented the band expanding. "We were locked into this sound and couldn't change," he explained. "The formula was embedded in everybody's minds. The protests I made fell on deaf ears... The public who liked our kind of records would not have gone that little bit further. We tested them, they wouldn't."

Scott's simple analysis of where a record buying public loses its commitment to an artist is a critique that may be applied to his career. In the sixties, Walker succeeded a generation of singers whose occupation was one of interpreting song. Before Sinatra, songs were largely delivered straight, and with little subjective biography injected into phrasing the lyric. If Billie Holiday was Sinatra's prototype in framing improvisations in reference to colouring the emotional character of the lyrics, then Sinatra who described his method as "saloon singing", was to add personal involvement to interpretation.

Scott began in a similar manner, and his first three solo albums combine interpretation with self-penned compositions. The concept of the singer/songwriter originated in the sixties, and the aim was largely financial. It is more lucrative for artists to record their own material, and whether or not they possess songwriting talents, this formula has become the observed protocol within the music industry. Scott differed from his vocal role-models by starting to write the songs he was to sing. *Scott* was also to include material written by Jacques Brel, Tim Hardin, and others, a pattern almost exactly repeated on *Scott 2*. The ratio of self-penned songs was to increase with each successive album, and to culminate in the entirely self-written *Scott 4*.

It was undoubtedly the ubiquitous rejection of *Scott 4* that contributed to Scott's resistance to undertake another entirely self-written project until the altogether weirder and menacingly up-ended *Climate Of Hunter*. By the time the artist came to record *Tilt*, his renewed sense of belief in himself, would have him say: "I wanted to make a nowhere record. I'd like people to sit and listen to it, get into it through the words. I'm looking for that Francis Bacon, in-the-face, whoops factor in the sound. And I get it sometimes."

Climate Of Hunter is riddled with drug references, a buried motif that resurfaces on *Tilt*. When Scott disappeared into mental space, after the commercial failure of *Scott 4*, and into temporary exile in Amsterdam, his distinct lack of motivation, and reported need to live constantly behind drawn curtains may have indicated a habit. The Scott Walker myth presents a number of tenable profiles, all of which revert back to an essentially insoluble enigma. In this, as I have commented, he entirely resembles Lautréamont. Whoever knew Lautréamont in Paris, at the time he was writing *Maldoror*, refused to break silence. There was no rumour, no sensation, no feedback about how the anomalous youth, Isidore Ducasse, had lived and died. His literary remains, *Les Chants de Maldoror* and *Poésies*, were all that survived him. That people at the time of his death, during the siege of Paris in November 1870, were feeding on cats, rats and dogs, only served to accentuate the bizarre circumstances surrounding his unexplained death.

The Scott legend seems almost as inviolable, and underpinned by the trust of friends who sanction his need for privacy. If isolation, and an increasing sequestration from the world in which he became a celebrity have been Scott's aims, then the man who comes out with a new record is almost in the unfortunate position of having to start all over again. Given the absence of singles, videos, or live promotion *Tilt* still achieved respectable credibility and watermarked at No. 30 in the British charts. Its comparative success suggests that the Scott Walker legend has over the decades recruited enthusiasts whose genuine respect for the artist extends to endorsing a work as obscure as *Tilt*. This was not the case with *Climate Of Hunter*, the latter proving a commercial disaster, although in retrospect it appears far more accessible than its successor. The time had been wrong for *Climate Of Hunter*. The unsuccessful Walker Brothers reformation in the late seventies, and the apparent absence of conviction surrounding that reunion, had implanted in Scott's audience the notion that he had lost his way. The Tom Rush ballad, "No Regrets", that he had so consummately lifted into the charts in 1976, had appeared vacuous in the light of his artistic development. The song appeared interchangeable with any number of MOR covers adaptable to the Walker voice.

By contrast, *Climate Of Hunter* with its lyric obscurity and entropic melodies seemed to present the uncovered wiring to Scott's psyche. Everything about the album resisted a resting point, and like

Tilt the songs offered the listener no comfortable pivot from which to reconstruct their meaning. Interviewed at the time of *Tilt* Scott was incisive about his method of using words as signs for altogether bigger states. "This isn't anything new, I've always done this," he will say. "It's just a way to talk about the unsayable things of existence, the unnameable. You're working around it, it's a lot of edge work. You're using language to discuss things that are beyond language."

Both *Climate Of Hunter* and *Tilt* appear in their context to be doing precisely that. *Tilt*, in particular, seems expressive of a complex emotional arena in which words are the subtext for a mood ensemble suggesting eschatological vision. In Scott's case, life has caught up with the need to record; the pressing exigencies of inner experience have demanded a form. This is what he means by knowing when it is the right time to make a new album. For Scott it's an inner thing, and if there's no compulsion to record, then he'll leave it alone. Even with his option taken up by Fontana, subsequent to *Tilt*'s critical success, Scott has made no immediate return to the studio, despite his expressed intentions to do so.

I think too that what Scott has been attempting to say over the years is that a man's work is the expression of a hard-won inner bias. At the time of his monumental success with the Walker Brothers, it was the image designed for the song that attracted fame. Over the years, and with the courage necessary for such a solitary undertaking, Scott has asked to be heard for his inner contents, rather than for the physical presentation of himself as a mediator between creativity and audience. On both *Climate Of Hunter* and *Tilt* we come close to reading Scott's inner dialogue as it touches on death and psyche. Commenting at the time of *Tilt*, on his youthful preoccupation with death as an aspect of creativity, he will say: "I don't think I've left that behind. I think I'm further into it. I felt it when I was younger in a very vertiginous kind of way, but this time it's more reconciliation, a weightier thing. I realised all the phenomena of existence very young and it was a hard thing for me. Now I'm living with it a little easier, more as an astonishment thing than a negative thing."

I want to go back to the notion of buried drug references in *Climate Of Hunter*. This particular work, as angular as it is to mainstream pop, is nonetheless a suite of songs that employ linear melody to greater effect than those which have to be coaxed out of *Tilt*. But the lyrics employ a private mythology of references from extreme psychic modalities, that suggests deep inner crisis. In "The Dealer", for instance, Scott sings, "Psalms of your hands/sung into the lateness/move a circuit on the white/and he can't feel a thing." The lyric is fraught with the desperate imagery of imploded withdrawal. Lines like, "Hissing brains boiling up press't to the bone/uncoils the wire whole night long" seem to find their analogue more with William Burroughs' fiction than with any element of Scott's work prior to *Climate Of Hunter*. The raw-nerved read-out of cellular war staged within the context of "The Dealer", may or may not suggest personal involvement, but it implies some sort of knowledge of smack withdrawal. I find this particular song one of the most disturbing that Scott has ever written, with its dispassionate insight into dysfunctional metabolism. Does this album hint at Scott kicking a habit, or am I reading a fiction into a fiction? Scott's terminology in "The Dealer", "keeping ice junkies packed hard on a seam", reads with the apparent authority of one who has been there.

Most anxiety states encompass a similar geography of panic. *Climate Of Hunter* may be likened to a map of these crisis points. Coming out of nowhere as the album did, the songs effect a sense of displacement and disorientation in the listener. The material is relayed with more urgency than the neutrally sustained phrasing on *Tilt*. The discomforting dynamic behind much of the material suggests a Scott on neural overload. The completely disembodied vocals on tracks like "Sleepwalkers Woman", provoke a poignancy in Scott's timbre in striking contrast to the often brutal lyrics. *Climate Of Hunter* explores an apocalyptic landscape of truncated bodies, shattered penitents looking to be blessed, drowned bodies, junkies, insomniacs, all of whom serve as metaphors for the modern city. In keeping with its experimental modality, four of the songs are left untitled, and just referred to by their track number in the sequence. Vision fireballs its way into "Track 3", the only song on the album thought sufficiently commercial to release as a single. Scott sings: "a miracle enters the streets, shining with rain/he is shaking to wash the murder away," as though the urban collective as much as the individual are guilty of some ineradicable crime. The imageries evoked by *Climate Of Hunter* meet a common web-site in the writings of Samuel Beckett, William Burroughs, and J.G. Ballard. Scott's method is to present his imageries as a series of film-frames, and his phrasing works with emphases to point up the narrative direction. In "Dealer", he will sing: "The other side/of a prowler/the dead/still search/the living," giving us the sort of imaginative quantum shifts that belong to film. It says much for Scott's vocal genius that he manages on both *Climate Of Hunter* and *Tilt* to phrase complex word-clusters within an emotional pitch. *Climate Of Hunter* was revolutionary as a pop album in that it made no least compromise on the artist's part towards his public. Even David Bowie's slabs of avant-garde experimentalism on *Low*, and *Heroes*, by way of Brian Eno's ambient perorations, had still retained half an album each of recognisable Bowie songs. The uniform abstruseness of Scott's lyric writing on *Climate Of Hunter*, together with intentionally withheld melodies makes it modern at the expense of Bowie's work which appears simply experimental.

The studio technique which Scott hinted as being instrumental to the making of *Tilt*, was presumably a method that held good for *Climate Of Hunter*. Without offering expansive insight into his working methods, Scott will volunteer: "By the time I get to the studio, it's all written down. I have to have readers I can work with, because I always want the music to be played together, at once. I don't want any drum machines or click tracks. Nothing like that. Very little overdubbing, if possible. I never try to give them too much indication of what I'm going to do. Because then it'll turn into a group thing, which isn't what I want either. I want each piece to have an intensity of its own. So it has a kind of febrile quality..."

Complete mastery of his sound has always been a Walker characteristic. There's the feeling with each of his solo-constructed albums that the conceptualised master is carried in his unconscious before being downloaded in the studio. The sound is cut clean from his head. It's a method executed on his first four solo albums, and a pattern repeated on his late trilogy.

On *Scott 3*, Walker had delivered a classily impish version of Jacques Brel's "Funeral Tango", a song in which the narrator presumes all manner of possibilities for his eventual death. It was a lighter and more acerbically ironic piece than Brel's altogether more sombre "My Death", which Scott had included on his first album. "Funeral Tango" fitted perfectly with the omnipresent death-wish in Scott's work, and the song title is almost a metaphor for the metaphysical combat Scott has staged with absolutes over the years. The man who accounted for one of his lengthy absences from recording by saying that he had been sitting around for years watching people play darts in bars, was no matter his distractions engaged in profound inner crises. The Virgin deal that Scott signed in February 1980, for a reported advance of £20,000, and a contractual agreement to deliver eight albums, was realistically undertaken by the artist to relieve him of financial pressures. Scott's back catalogue had been deleted by Phonogram, and with the capital lost in the abortive GTO deal that had resurrected the Walker Brothers, he had found himself living perilously close to the edge. Forced at one stage to sell off his voluminous record collection, Scott's deal with Virgin came as a veritable life-saver. That it took him four years to deliver an album that scarcely exceeds thirty minutes is indicative of Scott's off the wall inner dilemmas, and not of his inability to record. According to Scott's biographers, Mike Watkinson and Pete Anderson, Simon Draper, Virgin's managing director at the time, had several bizarre meetings with Scott to ascertain why he was so reluctant to record. At one meeting Scott was to claim that he could only record in May, as the regenerative forces of nature coincided with his creative cycle. At another discussion he claimed that the noise generated beneath his Kensington flat by a Virgin Help Organisation for unmarried mothers, was depriving him of the concentration needed to write.

It's clear that Scott's finely attuned neurology has become increasingly sensitive over the years to the inner and outer events that sanction his creativity. There's a degree of paranoid social estrangement in his relations with Virgin that suggests a man living on the cutting edge of himself. A decade later in his liner notes to *Boy Child*, a compilation put out to punctuate Scott's deepening silence and alienation from the music industry, Marc Almond was to note: "His voice has become a simile for all crooning deep tones and liquid vibrato – but there is only one Scott Walker: only he can create that special magic, the rest of us can only listen from the sidelines, learning to be content with our own individual characteristics..."

While Almond was in part refuting charges that his singing style on *The Stars We Are* (1988), was an attempt to emulate Scott's inimitably extended notes, he was also drawing attention to the dichotomy that existed, between Scott's legacy and his absence. At the time of Almond's writing, the only glimpse caught of Scott in the eighties was his brief cameo on a Britvic 55 television commercial. Other than that, he was presumed to have abandoned music, or to be attempting to secure a deal with an independent.

Scott who had turned down Virgin's option to record an album of covers, as an attempt to recoup the losses encountered by *Climate Of Hunter*, elected silence as his continuing role throughout the eighties. The relationship of silence to a singer is a profoundly critical one. Scott could presumably have covered the repertoire endorsed by Frank Sinatra, and Tony Bennett, or have interpreted contemporary songwriters, but his gravitation to silence was a stronger compulsion. From this we deduce that he is a reluctant voice, and not a singer like Sinatra for whom there is pleasure in bending notes, and achievement in the interpretation of song. Live performance has always been something that Scott has endured, meaning that his love of singing is less than his fear of an audience. In a 1996 Radio 2 Arts Programme, presented by Alan Clarke, Dave Dee who had toured with the Walker Brothers in 1965, told of how before a show Scott would sit in the dressing room, totally incommunicative, his head buried in his hands, and manifestly not wishing to be there. This vignette of the singer's agonized, backstage introversion, is supported by Scott's own admission that he turned down offers to perform at the Royal Albert Hall in 1970, due to unmodifiable stagefright.

I want to re-uptake the concept of silence and creativity. In reconsidering *Scott 4*, Walker will say: "*Scott 4* tried to link lyrics by Sartre, Camus and Yevtushenko to Bartok modal lines, but nobody noticed." Scott's referencing two philosopher/novelists, and major intellectuals, one poet and a classical composer is a tall cocktail of integrants. His resignation to the fact that "nobody noticed" suggests that we the listener, edit out what we don't hear. If we return to the record with Scott's exegesis at hand, we may discover these influences in the work. They are silent to the listener, until being activated by neurological noise.

Scott's silence, as he has described it in relation to *Tilt*, is characterised by waiting. When we go inward, which is the direction of looking for the creative field, we encounter silence. It's the necessary accompaniment to listening. Scott's silence is the inner stuff of which he is composed. He can choose to go into it or stay out. Making that silence heard is for him the process of making a record.

In his book *The Queen's Throat*, arguably the best thing ever written on voice, Wayne Koestenbaum speaks of records as having the ambivalent qualities of degeneration and regeneration. We can keep Scott in mind, when reflecting on Koestenbaum's observation that: "Records are tokens of disappearance and comeback; they are also portraits. I think of records as the degenerating portrait of Dorian Gray in Oscar Wilde's 1891 novel. A record pretends to be a boundaried, attractive, flattering portrait. But its instabilities, its mysteries, its potentially horrific features, need to be quarantined. The portrait annexes the soul of its beholder and grotesquely mutates. The portrait is vampiric. It doesn't keep a secret. It blurts out vices."

Scott seems far too aware of the degenerative potential of voice. His dissociation from his early work is part of the attempt to revoke an unwipeable fingerprint. Hearing himself then is an intrusion on silence. How he will sound is programmed into the silence he is experiencing now in his Bayswater apartment.

I'd like to stay with Kostenbaum's text for the space of another paragraph, and reflect on his apprehensions of how a record like a poem is only an approximation of the artist's intention. Kostenbaum writes: "A record can't limit the voice's meaning; a voice, once recorded, doesn't speak the same meanings that it originally intended. Every playing of a record is a liberation of a shut-in meaning – a movement, across the groove's boundary, from silence into sound, from code into clarity. A record carries a secret message, but no one can plan the nature of that secret, and no one can silence the secret once it has been sung."

Koestenbaum's series of insightings seems more than pertinent to Scott Walker. That a voice can't ever fully convey a singer's input is particularly relevant to *Tilt*. The tone of Scott's voice on the track, "Farmer In The City", and the feel of skeletal songs like "Tilt", and "Rosary", suggest a whole biography that's left unsaid. The singer who privately hired the Islington Town Hall, prior to recording *Climate Of Hunter*, in order to discover if he still had a singing voice, is clearly an artist who expresses little confidence in his voice. What does Scott hear when he listens to himself? He presumably encounters the same sense of unnerving disillusionment as writers do on re-reading past work. It's the wish to transcend himself has Scott live without copies of his work past or present. Only in that way can he occupy a silence that in turn leads to the resumption of creativity.

Within the pop milieu, success is usually dependent on available biography. Pop stars court media attention, so that the lifestyle appears to complement the work. But with Scott the reverse process accounts for his recognition. Nothing of his life is made public, and so the work is its sole representative. And ultimately it's the work that lives. Scott's quiet affirmation in foregrounding his creativity through the release of occasional albums is both a heroic gesture, and a statement of the honesty associated with the real thing. The voice speaks for itself.

In the Radio 2 Arts Programme devoted to Scott in 1996, his former manager Ed Bicknell commented on how Scott, "has the least interest in money of anyone I have met on this earth." The idea of creativity being synonymous with money has never entered Scott's precinct. There's the genuine feeling that *Tilt* exists as the vehicle for the artist's inner struggle, and not as a product calculated for a potential market. Speaking to Richard Cook at the time of *Climate Of Hunter*'s release, Scott spoke of the indigence he had experienced in and around that time. "I was trying to get some studio work on the quiet," he related, "but I didn't know who to go to... I was pretty broke. I had a bad history – I'd lost three flats just as I was gaining any kind of impetus – but they said at least start talking to Virgin again. I didn't know if that was the problem – they didn't realise I had to have money to complete it."

Scott has slipped in and out of perilous finances over the decades, re-blooded at times by a publisher's cheque or refloated by royalties from a Phonogram retro compilation. It was the unanticipated and phenomenal success in 1992 of *No Regrets/The Best Of Scott Walker And The Walker Brothers*, which again redeemed Scott's finances, and triggered the long overdue reissue of his first four solo albums on CD. Little or nothing of this appears to have influenced his creative cycle, and he has resolutely continued to avoid live performance as a source of income.

When in 1995, as part of the briefest promotion of *Tilt*, Scott broke a twenty years live abstinence by appearing on both *The Late Night Show*, and the Jools Holland show to sing "Rosary", the spectacle was an intensely harrowing one. Accompanying himself on electric guitar, eyes closed behind obligatorily defensive shades, Scott's whole organism appeared be the psychophysical instrument on which the song was played. Excruciatingly nervous, dressed without occasion for the stage, visibly leaning into himself and away from the viewing eye, Scott had never looked so flinchingly overexposed in the lights. But the pained intensity of his delivery, and the disembodied aspect to the voice presented a clip that is awesome in its relay of psychic anxiety. To sustain this level of emotional input over a full-length concert would be impossible, and despite Scott's intimating that he would perform *Tilt* live at the Queen Elizabeth Hall, the suggestion seems always to have been intended to remain a fantasy. Scott's brief, three-minute appearances on both shows manifested the strain of an individual who lives largely in inner space, abdicating that precinct for external contact. It looked like the singer had vacated his own planet, and was having difficulties in adjusting to studio reality.

The exercise if nothing else, suggested that legends are real. Scott Walker had succeeded in both shows in momentarily demythicizing the concept of absence surrounding his name. He had given note that he is present and contained by private space.

"It's an indecision, a grey area of vocal I want to produce," Scott had stated in relation to *Tilt*. Whatever colour Scott was searching to retrieve from his phrasing spectrum in the live take of "Rosary", the colour seemed to emerge as a prickly, angular charcoal. The notes are never expanded into his familiar cobalt register, but turn on wasteland territory, and are too anxious to settle. His phrasing foreshortens any possible trajectory of a baritone ceiling. The song is kept low and menaces at head-height. It's a survivor's song, but one which exists by the resolution to sing.

In the course of life we outgrow ourselves. It's this cushioning realisation that makes death possible. If we stayed identifying with a single mental construct, then we wouldn't relinquish youth or its ties. Scott's refusal to be located within his past suggests that he has adapted to growing older. It's probably not an issue with him, for any form of creativity lives in the continuous present.

Backtracking to August 6, 1967, when Scott performed his first solo set at the Fiesta Club in Stockton to the accompaniment of Ronnie Scott's band, he had on that occasion successfully brought together covers, his own material, and songs written by Jacques Brel. Dressed in a black mohair suit, and with his hair bleached, both concessions to the audience, Scott's palpable nervousness had been communicable to the cabaret audience. By 1995, his anxiety had grown transparent. If the cause was the same – the need to keep private his inner preoccupations – then the "Rosary" appearances confirmed the man's deepening in proportion to his work. In his 1995, *NME* interview, Scott in a semi-relaxed mood, illuminated something about his growing older: "But the terror thing is more important now than ever before because it is in some way bound up with your particular existence, and you have to see it through. And you have to take your listeners with you. Why should they be spared? You drag them into hell with you."

But I think what Scott is saying above all, is that if the work is extraordinary then it's a mark of the individual's inner development, and not a criterion for how they live in the external world. Scott's days are likely to be as ordinary as anyone else's; it's in their inner quality that the work is reflected. Brooding on his past at the time of *Tilt*, he will say: "I had a lot of self-loathing. I don't have a revenge factor. I'm not a saint, but I don't hold grudges or anything like that. But I did have self-loathing, and you can just get that in general. It can infiltrate every part of your life, so you've got to really work to keep it under control. I still get self-loathing now. Something just comes over you."

Self-loathing is damaging to creativity in that it prevents the artist having sufficient belief in himself to write or record. The Scott whose dynamic had something to prove in the making of his first three solo albums, was someone who hadn't yet experienced rejection. Even if the Walker Brothers had been dislodged from grace with a gradual decline in the chartability of their singles, they were still in 1967, a huge force with which to contend. Scott had surfed that success in his early solo career, and was only to begin to lose his committed fan-base in 1970. During this period the psychological aspects of self-loathing had been suppressed due to the optimistic momentum of his career.

The individual who surfaced for interviews at the time of *Climate Of Hunter*, and again for *Tilt*, was someone whose legend was in need of new work to support its claims. The inconsistencies, and apparent lack of base to Scott's output in the seventies, his flirtation with country music having largely gone ignored, had left him susceptible to vitiated self-esteem. Apart from the praise singled out for 1978's "The Electrician", Scott's output in the seventies had been considered a series of misjudged attempts to re-start a faltering career. There was all this talent and it was existing in silence. There was all this voluminous potential without the focus of a studio.

Adverse criticism, no matter an artist's self-defences, has a

---

deleterious effect on the soul. The blackness festers and may lead to self-doubt or feelings of dejection. But however poorly *Climate Of Hunter* may have sold, the critical reception in the face of its oddity was sufficient to sustain Scott through the decade's silence ended by *Tilt*. At least a redeeming bridge on which the artist could balance, had been slung over the abyss.

Scott clearly tangos with his inner antagonists. He has expressed his deep feelings of frustration at having wasted the seventies, but he seems little perturbed by the time that has elapsed between *Climate Of Hunter* and *Tilt*. He seems satisfied that one has grown out of the other, and that the two pursue his genre of expression to its extremes. *Climate Of Hunter*'s essentially imploded terrain had suggested that a follow up would prove impossible. By making *Tilt*, which is the closest thing to sonic millenarianism that we will get, Scott has suggested that his talents are extensible again.

The end of a second meeting within this essay. Scott's Radio 2 Arts Programme ends with the words, "We never knew the man. We may have been close to him, but nobody knew Scott." I'm looking for the man inside the work. The man in shades, a quilted green anorak, baseball hat and blue denims may be out meeting a friend this moment. I'll never know, and you'll never know; but we can meet the enigma each time we choose to listen to his songs. It's then that Scott comes out of hiding. Not in Bayswater, but in your room.

SLEEPWALKERS WOMAN

There's a popular belief, and one in part endorsed by Scott himself, that the last two albums he cut before leaving Philips are inferior to their predecessors. I am of course referring to the albums, *The Moviegoer* (1972), and *Any Day Now* (1973). The dismissal of these albums is not a critical consensus with which I hold. The fact that both comprise covers, and are both largely ballad albums has led to their consistently pejorative assessment.

Scott Walker is not an artist to consider minor songs. Both albums find Scott in superlative voice, and while the records may lack subjective input – Scott is not in this case singing about himself – they are nonetheless coloured by accomplished vocal finesse. Nobody was blaming Sinatra in 1973 for not sensationalising his life through self-penned lyrics. There is surely an interpretative aesthetic, whereby the singer's art resides in the voice, per se, and Scott's excursions into covers enhanced his idiosyncratic sensitivity to lyric. Scott's melody lines had sustained him well in his song-writing on his first three albums, but his melodies on *Scott 4*, and *Til The Band Comes In*, had sounded invariable and lacking in contrasts. The Scott formula had at the time been overworked with decreasing memorability. What Scott regained on *The Moviegoer*, and *Any Day Now*, was necessary variety and a corresponding set of vocal metamorphoses which extended even to the reggae-based "Maria Bethania", on *Any Day Now*. Scott's execution of the latter song makes it something of a vocal template for how he was to instrumentalise his voice on *Tilt*.

What I'm saying is that these two albums represent stages of development in Scott which were to result in the unorthodox genius responsible for the apocalyptic survivalism manifested on *Tilt*.

Scott's delivery of the blue-mooded Bacharach/Hillard composition, "Any Day Now", is as fine as any of his middle-blue spectrum songs. The mood evoked sounds like cinema-bleu, and the

---

song is grounded in late afternoon in Scott's perfectly modulated register. The song has me think of a lover in deep thought and uncertainty, crossing town at the hour "when blue shadows fall". There's every justification for this song being included on a 'Best Of Scott' compilation. There are other outstanding successes on *Any Day Now*, amongst them a hypersensitive reading of the David Gates song, "If", on which Scott floats his notes into the empyrean. His rendition of this song is so marvellously constructed as to serve as a model for voice-coaching, and the absence of vibrato has the song stand as a fingerprint of the Walker voice. The sort of critical disparagement that lives as a saturnine ring over *The Moviegoer*, and *Any Day Now*, owes its origins in part to Scott's frustrated dismissal of albums that were unenthusiastically received at the time of their release. Scott not only selected the songs, but at the time of recording them imparted his vocal-seal to their living potential.

That the material coincided with the bisexual advent of glam rock, and David Bowie, in no way deletes its importance. It would be hard to listen to interpretations as perfect as the histrionic "The Ballad Of Sacco And Vanzetti", from *The Moviegoer*, or the transparent reading of Jimmy Webb's "If Ships Were Made To Sail", from *Any Day Now*, without feeling Scott's voice pointing up its optimum baritone. The voice showcased on these albums is as near to the greats like Sinatra, as Scott ever achieved in an interpretative genre.

Some of the misconceptions surrounding Scott's albums of covers were instigated by his saying in retrospect: "If they wanted me to do movie themes, I would pick the best movie themes I thought were possible and I would do them – Sinatra-type stuff. I'll imitate anybody. It was down to that. Whatever needed to be done."

But it was never that simple, and to assume that Scott was volitionless in his choice of material as the shaping tool of his future is to do an injustice to his integrity. Songs like "Do I Love You", and "When You Get Right Down To It", from *Any Day Now*, and "The Summer Knows", and "Come Saturday Morning", from *The Moviegoer* are distinct inner readings of commendable material. The songs differed little in surface quality from the covers on his first solo album, numbers that included "When Joanna Loved Me", "Through A Long And Sleepless Night", and "You're Gonna Hear From Me".

It was more that the critical climate had gone against ballad singing, particularly when it was complemented by high romantic orchestration. The early hits scored by the Walker Brothers were lyrically less distinguished than much of the material Scott lifted into *bel canto* on *The Moviegoer*, but in chartable terms rock music had gained the ascendancy over pop ballads. At the time, Scott was considered to be exploiting an unfashionable medium, and the new zeitgeist of glam rock icons, Marc Bolan, David Bowie, and Lou Reed, had arrived as electric avengers on Scott's heroically orchestrated vocals. The idea that Scott's less fashionable work in the early seventies is indicative of lack of merit is an idea in need of revision. It was then, and has been subsequently assessed by a set of critical values demanding that it should be something other than what it is. The often maligned *Scott Sings Songs From His TV Series*, suffered from Scott's dismissal, "For me, the entire album is an exercise", but it is arguably his finest vocal album, no matter its being contra the image of the woundedly introspective singer who had presided over the early solo albums.

Scott's confusion throughout his first decade as a singer seems to have been provoked by the paradoxical dilemma raised by voice. He had committed himself, seemingly irrevocably, to a particular sound, and that sound had been substantiated by image. In the sixties, Scott had represented an image-voice, and the extraordinariness of that instrument had been commercially validated by the singer's looks and success. There was the feeling that the voice was superior to the material recorded, but at the same time there was the unconscious conviction that if the voice was removed from its formula, then it would be out of place, and unsuited to pop music. Scott's voice at the time seemed to have too many affinities with an older generation of standard singers, who before the easy listening revival were outlawed as Las Vegas anomalies. Scott's quandary was what to do with his voice. By the nature of its exceptional baritone register, the voice was overexposed by comparison with contemporaries. Scott's voice couldn't be hidden; it couldn't be made less than its worth, and it appeared embarrassingly odd in a pop milieu which had replaced voice with marketable image.

It seemed by the early seventies that Scott had exhausted the commercial possibilities available to his vocal spectrum within the pop ethos, and this was in turn to lead to his departure from Philips for CBS. His cobalt-rinsed, peak and fall pitched ballads had come to be associated with a sixties production sound that leant heavily on Phil Spector's earthquaking percussion.

Scott was left with no other option but to retreat into his inner silence and wait for the conceptualisation of a new sound. The dense experimental textures that were to go into the making of *Climate Of Hunter*, and *Tilt*, were not available to the singer then, and instead he elected to use the predominantly country sound that pervades *Stretch* and *We Had It All*. This style meant using the voice in a different way on selective covers, and therefore lowering the ceiling of Scott's register. What Scott achieved in this role was to read country with amazing transparency, and to take it away from its more customary nasal delivery. Interviewed at the time of *Tilt*, Scott will backtrack to the prevailing ideologies that crossed the threshold of the sixties into the early seventies, and say: "I think it was just so silly. They really weren't prepared to go far enough. I realise everyone was naive, including myself. It's just that everything I was influenced by was being blown away by this inane attitude."

Scott's own writing largely constellates around in the mind songs, that is material conceived from subjective states, and demanding serious reflection on the part of the listener. It's what happens on both *Climate Of Hunter* and *Tilt*. The material goes into you and you go into the material. In the early seventies Scott seems to have let that idea go, and to have asked that his singing voice should stand as the criterion by which he should be judged. It's not the material he recorded or how he recorded it that is suspect, it's more his own communicated reservations about using song as a form of expression in itself, that put him at odds with his measured eloquence on this material.

There are superlative ballad renditions on both of Scott's so-called country albums, and perhaps none finer than "Sundown" on *We Had It All*. A brooding song concerning guilt over acts committed "in a room where you do what you don't confess", the dramatics of the material seemed tailored to Scott's mystique. At the time of the album's release, Scott was to say: "In my opinion it has what I had on the first two or three solo albums – it has the conviction that I lost, and I think by the time I get my writing into the framework I'll have achieved the circle again." Conviction is a big part of singing, and Scott brings his inner contents to the material. That his new slant proved uncommercial at the time, is in no way a reflection on the voice that coloured the songs. Scott's affinities with country had been manifest on his first two solo albums, where he had looked to Tim Hardin for the fragile miniatures, "The Lady Came From Baltimore", and "Black Sheep Boy".

Scott's vocal treatments of the standards on his two CBS albums are right up there with his optimum performances. That these songs have also lived under a penumbra of critical indifference in no way does them justice. They are not just simplistic interpretations of standards, they are songs touched by Scott's particular sensitivity. Again, the error comes from assessing them in terms of chartable merit. "Just One Smile" from *Stretch* is sung with a filigree sensitivity to hurt. It's as good a take of a pain-ballad as Scott has ever achieved, the voice coming in to stark piano accompaniment, and turning the lyric on a fineness that foregrounds the singer's emotions. Scott had never sounded so careful in his phrasing.

Scott was also in part the victim of transitional decades. The emphasis on youth culture as the dynamic generated by sixties and seventies pop, also had a generation unwilling to countenance the stylised vocals of Sinatra and his alumni. Their method was seen as unhip. Scott's problem after his early iconisation with the Walker Brothers was that when he attempted to sing ballads straight, and removed from pop arrangements, then he risked being categorised with the Sinatra generation of crooners.

There are other outstanding takes on *Stretch*, and amongst them a poignantly phrased "Someone Who Cared", where again Scott takes his cue from a piano and delivers with a feeling tone that keeps him in a familiar blue spectrum. His reading of the song, which could have been one of his own in its compassionate evocation of regret at having let life slip by, balances right on a perfect edge. You get the feeling that nobody else could have done this, and that it's there for ever.

When Scott compared the feeling quality of his work for CBS to the emotional input he had given to his first three albums, he was right to make the comparison. His treatment of the songs on *Stretch*, and *We Had It All*, explores the same area in psyche which he had chosen to locate on the early triumvirate of solo albums. The voice at once searchingly tender, and experientially grained with pain, isolates the phrasing with a disarmingly vulnerable clarity. The listener warms to the apparent feel of the singer's emotional contents. You can get to understand a great deal about the intrinsic Scott Walker, if you pay careful attention to the singing voice on *Stretch*, and *We Had It All*. They are albums on which the voice coaxes the maximum sensitivity from the lyrics. They are voice models with a roomy psychic interior.

Disappearance in terms of Scott's refusal to entertain past achievements is of course an existential realisation of freedom. But the failure to own to a past leads to an inevitable rupture in continuity. At the time of his *Tilt* interviews, Scott will question: "It's so crazy to me. You get unbelievable, or even believable people being picked up all the time who aren't selling records. It's puzzled me. People expect a lot more sales out of me than are generated. So they're vastly disappointed. Whereas with other artists they'll eke it out."

Scott is indirectly referring here to Virgin's disappointment at the low sales generated by *Climate Of Hunter*. It's in part the legend surrounding Scott's name that is responsible for anticipated sales; and his discontinuous momentum that prevents their happening. There's an inevitable suspicion attached to the motivation informing a new Scott Walker album. If we associate his prolonged silences with disinterest in singing, or disrespect to his following, then the reason behind a creative return will always be questioned. On the interview CD that Scott prepared for *Tilt*, he tells us that the conception of an album from the time of writing to the time of executing the schema in the studio occupies a period of two and a half years. Scott who was notorious even during his brief residency with CBS, for being late to deliver, seems obstinately unwilling to hurry the process. Time as we associate it with achieved doing, is very different from the imaginal space of being occupied by the creative artist. We can imagine Scott blasting his way back to creativity through alcohol, as a means of attacking suppressed energies.

Lovers of Scott as a blue-mooded texturist will pick up on "Stormy", a mid-tempo, bruisy cover included on *Til The Band Comes In*, which is effectively *Scott 5*. Scott thought sufficient of the song to include it in his live repertoire at Fagin's in Manchester in 1973. A one time hit for Classic IV, "Stormy" is the sort of broody, left out in the rain song that isolates the rejected lover in a way that suited Scott's wounded persona at the time. If "Stormy" had been a self-penned track, it would have been marked up for attention, but Scott's covers, excluding his versions of Brel, have always attracted critical disparagement. "Stormy" is short in the way of sixties pop songs, but over a pronounced bass-line, Scott discovers the loneliness at the song's interior. A vignette-lyric that tells the story of a rejected lover who calls his departed girlfriend, "Stormy", Scott reads the song with the measured gravity of someone who coaxes mood from the lyrics. "Stormy" in Scott's rendition is companionable to blue moods, and is read light-sensitive to the broken hearted. So many of Scott's inimitable covers have been consigned to critical neglect, as though they are epiphenomenal to his real creativity. "Stormy" sounds to me as good a mood song as Scott ever recorded, and right up there with a better accepted cover of his, "In My Room". Voice and arrangement treat the song filmically, so that the lovers' separation is placed in the visual imagination, a landscape of lowering blueblack skies shot through with intermittent sunlight.

"Stormy", as a highlight track also suffered neglect due to its inclusion on an album for which nothing happened. "People listened to the first track which was an instrumental and thought: 'Oh, here he goes again... gloomy Sunday'. The sort of material I have been writing just isn't a saleable product. I wasn't disappointed because I knew it wouldn't sell." Scott's comments at the time of the release of *Til The Band Comes In*, suggested a resignation to his having been waste-landed in a non-commercial zone.

Pop artists were considerably more prolific in the sixties than their latterday contemporaries. An artist's career was presumed to be short-lived, and so output was immediate. There wasn't a long-term overview as to the durability of the work, and Scott who had achieved two Top Ten albums in 1969, was after the failure of *Scott 4*, and *Til The Band Comes In*, the latter belonging to 1970, considered to have peaked. To a sixties industry the failure to maintain a commercial profile was tantamount to artistic suicide. The image-fixated teenagers who had elevated the Walker Brothers to a transient demi-god apogee in the pop world, were no longer interested in Scott's intellectually conceptualised music. Quite suddenly a black hole had appeared and Scott had stepped into it. Unfortunately for Scott, all his misgivings about the artificial premises on which pop fame were founded appeared to have been confirmed. The audience who had instated him as a sex symbol had deserted him as an artist. In a very real way Scott considered himself never to have been heard. Scott had attempted in each of his first six solo albums to incorporate material that lifted him out of a pop matrix, and contrasted his avant-garde sympathies with his generic role as a ballad singer. To go only with Scott's self-penned compositions is to deny his singularity of voice.

Back to "Stormy", and the mood association with rain. Rain is the element most present in songs written to evoke solitude, blueness and unrequited love. Scott's tonal emphasis on the word "rain" speaks worlds for the film noir lonely, and also for the isolated and outlawed in cities. His own song, "It's Raining Today", from *Scott 3*, is a blue-hearted anthem to the solitary who feel their alienation increased by staccato rainfall. The Walker Brothers had addressed rain in their cover of "Walking In The Rain", and the theme has been a consistent mood-signifier in Scott's balladic oeuvre. The romantically down-mooded Scott personified by his work between 1967–1970, is both the image and the reality of someone whose introspective life was consolingly orchestrated by the sound of night rain. Rain is a comforter to those whose inner wounds need healing. "Stormy" is one of Scott's great rain songs. Scott, Marc Almond, and Billie Holiday all seem by the manner of their singing to invite rain into their songs. Marc Almond's song, "Untitled", is complementary in its rainy, nocturnal aspects to Scott's sonorously daytime "It's Raining Today". It doesn't rain in "Big Louise" or "Montague Terrace In Blue", but both songs appear to invite storm clouds. "Always Coming Back To You" is similarly roofed with blue-grey presentiments of a rain sky.

There's also an element of brown in Scott's early tonal repertoire. I say that not just because he recorded Jimmy Webb's "Where Does Brown Begin" on *Stretch*, but because of his propensity to incorporate some of the big American spaces into his country material, and traces of those brown terrains follow all the way through to the title song on *Tilt*, with its inclusion of buffalo in the song's schema. Interviewed in 1995, Scott will explain the constituents of "Tilt" as: "I can only say that it's satirical. It's a kind of black country music song. I structured the chords very carefully through the whole album and there are new chords. The chords in 'Tilt' are meant to be a yin and yang thing. David Rhodes is actually playing a major and a minor at the same time... It's a country song that becomes my own vision of something else during the key change. That's all I can say."

"My own vision of something else", is of course the essence of true singing, and by that I mean the transformation that happens inwardly to the singer in the course of delivery. Reading a song should find its analogue in writing a poem, and be the expansion of something preconceived into an autonomous take-over that surprises the artist. What you begin with alters radically in the field of conception. And this applies to both Scott's self-compositions and his covers. The trajectory of the song is dependent on mood, emotional colouring, and a whole network of subtle energies which go to inform the voice. There would be something very wrong if a singer wasn't surprised by the outcome of a song. In a talk on the poet, William Blake, Allen Ginsberg concluded his paper with the sentiment, "Blake was astonished by his own imagination". This assumption should hold good for a singer in the way it rings true for a poet. When Scott is in voice, he will surprise himself.

The psyched quality of Scott's voice, which implies soul in pitched tone, is abundantly evident in the cover "When Joanna Loved Me" from *Scott*. Scott's version of this song competes for a higher place than Tony Bennett's superlative execution of the number, by reason of psyche. It's not just the rotundity of Scott's vocal ceiling that fingerprints the lyrics, it's the tremblingly sensitive empathy he feels with the regret that comes of loss of love, that has him claim the song for his own. "When Joanna Loved Me" seems to fit Scott's violet spectrum, partly because the song is set in Paris, and the season evoked is spring. His voice on this song is a redemptive instrument, and one that seems to pull Joanna out of the crowd, and out of yesterday. In the course of delivering the song Scott seems to make possible the miracle of retrieving dead love. While the singer can't alter the song's meaning, he can bend its possibilities, and Scott achieves this rare instance on "When Joanna Loved Me".

Nobody has written about the intrinsic dynamic behind Scott's voice, and that's because in part voices are secret, and inhabit silence. The inner music that goes into the writing of a poem finds its correlative in how a singer listens to internal instructions. It's from that inner place that the song will find its directive.

"It's strange," Scott will say in 1995, "because everybody says

– people who aren't particularly into what I'm doing now – why don't you make another Walker Brothers record? I don't think anyone would be that interested, quite honestly." The lack of authenticity that would generate a revamped Walker Brothers – Scott's deepening inner silence wouldn't answer the voice call – would be much like their unsuccessful seventies reunion. Scott's inner journey has taken him a long way from singing to order.

Over the years Scott appears to have achieved an overview on the various musical components which have gone into his making, and to have brought them to a summation in the recording of *Tilt*. It probably doesn't feel like that to him when he's painting, out at the supermarket, unable to write, or generally having a blue day. Achievements disappear then, and despondent feelings of neglect or self-failure take over. When an artist isn't in the lights, he invariably feels forgotten. Cult artists are cited as influences, and become part of the subliminal thrust of a genre, but they're also backgrounded into subculture. But Scott Walker is a cult artist by reason of artistic integrity, and not through the inability to be popular. He has known popularity and rejected it as a fool's cardboard crown. No amount of Walker Brothers reunions would be worth the solid mastery of *Climate Of Hunter* and *Tilt*. Scott works with the secrecy of an alchemist, transmuting base matter into gold, or the shadow aspects of psyche into light. His voice celebrates the completion of the work.

Let's look at some contrasting components in Scott's work. For instance, the superb timing and unearthly resonance that the singer imparts to "Angelica" from *Scott*, represent Scott meeting himself through a sympathetic cover. The voice on "Angelica" is him at his best. When he sings, "I passed a flower shop, Lord knows I meant to stop", you feel the admission go right through you. It's something we've all done, and it reflects the uncertainty we may feel about showing love. We should have arrived with a statement of blood-red roses, but we let the opportunity go. The name "Angelica" may be substituted for whatever the listener's date may happen to be called. In other words, accessibility allows the listener to step direct into the song's arena. "Angelica" is a vocal triumph, but seems to have merited little attention amongst Scott's anthologers. It's romantic, baroque, purple, and sung with the intention to raise a ceiling on romantic lyrics. The claim Scott makes on "Angelica" is heartfelt. Within the context of the song the two are lovers.

Neither *Climate Of Hunter*, nor *Tilt*, provides that sort of personalised relationship between the voice and its subject. The characters on both of these later albums are more abstractly sketched, and are cues for Scott's inner concerns. The endgame refugees of his unconscious allow for no intimate bonding between listener and voice. Scott has in a way outgrown character singing. The beautiful personal relationship he established on another name song, "Joanna", brought summer and a sense of bittersweet longing for a lost girl into the listener's private space. Scott got the whole visual complement on "Joanna" direct into his voice texture. "Angelica", "Joanna", "Mathilde", and "Genevieve", are names that Scott has brought alive in the romantic repertoire.

In the eighties, as a gesture on Virgin's part to fire the inactive Scott into studio enthusiasm, collaborations were mooted with Brian Eno, Daniel Lanois and David Sylvian. Eno and Lanois got down to preparing backing tapes for the reluctant Scott, who in turn considered their treatments too clinically technological. Scott has never moved away from the desire to have organic instruments colour his voice. Scott's creative ethos is one involving spiritual combat, and sophisticated software wouldn't in his eyes do justice to the rich components of voice. In this way he has remained true to live sound, and the singer's aspecting of vulnerability as part of song. Of his proposed collaboration with David Sylvian, Scott will say: "He's much more of an ethereal merchant than I am. I'm a man who struggles with spirituality, whereas he's given into it. My album and the one before it are about struggle in a Dostoyevskian sense. It's a real fight for me in every line. Whereas he's given in to a state of grace."

Scott is in fact on *Climate Of Hunter*, and *Tilt*, singing against the grain. The Dostoyevskian struggle of which he speaks is evident in the way the singing voice appears to take its lead from spiritual crisis. On much of *Tilt*, the voice can be heard emerging from the abyss. It's a survivor's tone dominates, an almost pre-death admission of having seen and known before extinction. "Harness on the left nail," he sings on "Farmer In The City", acknowledging the difficulty of being. Everything owned to on *Tilt*, and its predecessor, sounds to have been hard won, in the way that such inner landscapes rarely become the subject of song. When the voice is totally isolated as it is on "Rosary", then its nakedness turns you over to face your own inner demons. Listening to *Tilt* should be a prompter to evaluating one's own inner contents.

"Singing is a terrifying thing for me," Scott will say on his *Tilt* Interview CD. "I want to get even the terror of the voice on the landscape," he will say in relation to "The Cockfighter". He will also talk of his method of trying to conceptualize the idea behind his vocal take as soon as he enters the studio. "I walk in and go straight over to the mike," he will say of his method, eliminating any conception we may have of him labouring over successive mixes. And of *Tilt*, he will say the album constitutes "a desire and a longing".

In the case of *Tilt*, Scott appears to have been eager to commit his pre-conceived sound to record, without distractions or embellishments. Part of the terror to which Scott refers lies in the reality of the time-frame in which recording takes place. There's the need to get it all down in the allocated studio time. His voice will fingerprint the DAT with his signature of the moment. Everything he has been over the twelve years since he last entered the studio will have to be organized around the voice. The experience will be one of awesome intensity and anticipation on Scott's part. "The lyric is dictating everything," Scott will say of the process, insisting that the chord structure of each individual song is dependent on the lyric bias.

It's a courageous method from which to work, and one that Scott has always pursued as an artist. Programmed software has come increasingly to bury the pop lyric in textured sound, and Scott's authorial isolation of meaningfully poetic lyric as the naked proponent of song is an act of heroic intention. It's sometimes hard to call the individual pieces on *Tilt* songs, for they appear as complex movements motivated by singular voice. In this way Scott crosses a devastated terrain as a voice-survivor. His tone appears at times to be instructing the damaged to rise and go on.

Speaking of *Tilt* in the prepared Interview CD, Scott will cite R.E.M's Michael Stipe as an example of someone who writes esoteric lyrics, and call his own an example of "extreme lucidity" by comparison. Scott's lyrics on *Tilt* exist by reason of the same ambiguity as their subject matter. They allude to the idea of things, and not to those things themselves.

Of his past work, Scott will say: "I think a lot of it was absolutely awful. That's not false modesty, its' absolutely true. It's the old story of the guy who made it seeing flaws. Some of it was very good. But the time I wasted after those first records was shameful."

Where does that place the artist? Presumably with his concerns shifted to face the present. Most committed works of creativity lose their shine to the subjectively orientated artist, once his or her preoccupations are organised around the new. Scott will probably always accept *Climate Of Hunter*, and *Tilt*, into his accepted achievements, but he will view both albums simply as stages towards realising another work in process.

It was Mark Edwards, who in the course of reviewing the Scott biography, *A Deep Shade Of Blue*, drew attention to a paradox in Scott Walker's career, which is tangential to aspects of my study. Edwards remarked that "his music was too serious for a pop audience, and far too pop for a serious audience." There is a truth in this observation that has continued to this day. *Tilt*, no matter its esoteric aspirations and anti-pop melodies, was still proclaimed by the pop ethos as a freakish incursion on post-modernism. That the record's string arrangements owe something to Scott's pop legacy, and the percussion to industrial sampling, helps to define *Tilt* as marginal pop, but its main thrust – the voice-use and the lyric landscapes explored by that voice – point more to minimalist theatre and film noir. The music is a fusion of the jazz, classical and pop that Scott has assimilated as purposeful to his genre. The components are mixed to emphasise the total alienation of man in the light of military dictators and political despots. Scott's cry is for the wounded individual in the face of totalitarianism.

All of this may seem a long way from the original boy meets girl scenario of fifties and sixties pop. Pop music has of course grown progressively more complex over the decades, but not to the degree that Scott has interiorized it on *Tilt*. The man has gone out to an edge, and is probably unaware of the creative outpost he occupies.

And so back to "Sleepwalkers Woman", and the idea of ghosting a landscape. The song proceeds circularly in the way of Dante's Inferno. "For the first time unwoken I am returned," Scott sings, charting through his voice the journey of a nocturnal exile. There's a marvellously surreal quality to lines like, "She will fold him away in his badly changed hand". The frozen terrain on which the couple in this song meet is one charged with nocturnal stillness. The lyric is shaved to the bone, like a poem by Paul Celan. The words are cut to the quick of being. You could imagine this woman having stepped out of a painting by Paul Delvaux.

Scott probably got the words down in another form, and then worked on it for voice, eliminating all excess. The Bob Carlos Clarke photo of Scott on the sleeve of *Climate Of Hunter*, depicts him characteristically caught between inner and outer modes of expression. The orchestrated sensitivity of the man is visible as he fractionally compromises in making a gesture with his hand, as though he is speaking. We know he isn't speaking, but that's the trick. Scott's inner awareness is being made public. He's half in and half out of his characteristic introspective resting-point. The same balance is achieved whenever he sings.

We're near the end of the third of our meetings with Scott through accessing his work. In the privacy of our homes we can bring him alive each time we listen to his voice. The availability can seem almost a voyeuristic intrusion. It's silent one moment, and then in the next Scott is filling the room with his hurt baritone. It's part of the pact of unconditional accessibility an artist makes in issuing a record. The finished product can be heard by anyone at any time, anywhere. Somebody on this diamond-pointed Friday afternoon may be searching out a Scott CD in one of the megastores. It always seems to be a Friday on which I find myself coming to a section ending in my meetings with Scott. In the process of writing he comes to companion the page. He's probably not doing anything today that's out of character. He may be reading, painting, thinking, or hitting the contents of his thoughts against a friend. Asked why he wouldn't perform *Tilt* live he will say: "My concern would be people coming along for the wrong reasons." He will expand this reservation into the notion that people may be wishing to hear him perform Walker Brothers material. Scott has no wish to confront himself out of context. He has no wish to deconstruct the present by referencing his past. Whatever he's doing now will contribute unconsciously in some way to the new work he's in the process of discovering. Rainy Fridays are partial endings to weeks. This chapter is one of them.

WHO (WILL TAKE MY PLACE)

Blue psychological types, by which I mean the melancholy aura which appears to invest certain types of artist, are often prototypical romantics whose ideals have been depressed by their life experience. Back in 1973, Philips put out a selection of songs under the title *The Romantic Scott Walker*. The album sleeve repeated the moody, black and white photograph of the singer to be found on *Scott*. Wearing dark glasses and a scarf, and with highlighted hair, the image portrays Scott in a moment of genuine anguish. He seems to be preoccupied with inner concerns. He is isolated in character. His troubled expression may be viewed in retrospect as indicative of the disquieting years to come, which were to chase him into a still deeper solitude.

The Romantic Scott Walker comprises one side of covers from *Scott Sings Songs From His TV Series*, and one side selected from *Scott*. It was the first time the epithet romantic had been married to Scott, although the unspoken reality of it had always existed in the singer's voice and aesthetic mystique, so too in the extraordinary looks with which he was endowed. Prominently featured on *The Romantic Scott Walker* is his evocatively pitched version of Brel's "My Death", a song counterpointed against the singer's youth, and so made more tragic by a young person's apprehension of death. Scott's autumnal approach to "My Death", "my death waits among the falling leaves, in magician's mysterious sleeves" is compounded of romantically insighting the prospects of death through a sensibility which appears to cajole its premature happening. Scott's palpable ethereality and seriousness became a song that at the time of his recording it in 1967, was a way of pushing his morbid preoccupations to extremes. It was at this stage of his career Scott's ultimate statement of appearing to value death above life. The singer seemed to have embraced Keats' notion of being "half in love with easeful death". "My Death" could have been written for Scott, and his reading of

Brel's dynamic addresses the lyric contents with an almost metaphysical sensitivity. In Scott's rendition the song serves as a metaphoric funeral for the passing of his youth. *Scott* was the transitional album necessary to extract the singer from direct associations with the pop milieu, and "My Death" was the register of Scott's leap into adulthood. Singing it was also an affirmation of the romantic ideal of love outliving death. The idea of death is made tolerable in Brel's lyric through the hope that love will be there to help the song's protagonist through the final door.

Scott, who at the time of recording "My Death", was blinding himself with whiskey in the Soho jazz clubs, and most notably at Ronnie Scott's, was twice reported to have been found unconscious, once in Soho, and once in a nocturnal Regents Park. Rumour was out that Scott was either a sexual outlaw, or an artist impulsed towards the tragic self-destruction of greats like Billie Holiday. Unable to sleep, and strung out with anxiety, the youthful Scott would take night walks to compensate for chronic insomnia. The idea of the traumatised singer out in the night-time Baker Street area of London, did much to enforce the image of the romantic Scott Walker. Scott's sensibility was considered too fine to cope with the ethos of stardom.

We consider romantic an artist who exalts the ideals of love and creativity in their opposition to time. The artist risks his mortality by attaching greater importance to imagination than to life itself. The pursuit of truth becomes the ideal for living. Romantics don't always die young. The poet W.B. Yeats, and the composer Wagner are instances of romantics who chased their respective visions into old age. The nineteenth century, was however, a burial ground for the early dead. The romantics who it claimed young, included Keats, Shelley, Byron, Lautréamont, Rimbaud, and Nietzsche. The deathcount continues into the twentieth century with the foreshortened lives of Delius, Modigliani, and D.H. Lawrence, right up to the eclipse of movie and pop icons like Marilyn Monroe, Jim Morrison, Jimi Hendrix, Brian Jones, and Elvis Presley. The world is left begging a talent that has been summarily removed. It's as though the flower has lacked the time to know its wintering.

In his youthful career Scott appeared to be targeted as a potential romantic suicide. Early songs with the Walker Brothers like "Saddest Night In The World", and the painfully wounded, "Young Man Cried", had suggested a singer so close up to his profiled material that death would prove the only release from an obsessive preoccupation with the moribund. Scott who was visibly locked in an agonized world of spiritual tensions, seemed anxious to dissociate himself from his American upbringing, and to steep himself in European culture. He made no mention of his having been a child talent on Broadway, and was clearly embarrassed by the singles he had demoed at the ages of fourteen and fifteen, under the name Scotty Engel. This material recorded in the period of 1958/9, and subsequently released much to the singer's displeasure under the title, *Looking Back With Scott Walker*, in 1967, showed a precocious talent at too formative a stage to realise any artistic direction. Scott was also to say at the time of recording his first solo album: "My whole life revolves around my records... I only make just enough money to get by. I suppose you could call it a hand-to-mouth existence." The romantic ideal that Scott pursued at this time, has seemingly changed little over the years, and depends on an axis that places the conviction of truth above that of compromise for commercial gain. The artist who made *Tilt* is the same inflexible perfectionist in pursuit of a vision, as the young man who recorded *Scott*, and spoke of "waiting for my speck of dust to shine".

Mario Praz's book *The Romantic Agony*, is a vast compendium of the author's speculative theories relating to creative pathologies. In writing of Charles Baudelaire, Praz suggests, "he does not aim at astonishing the reader's mind, but rather at shocking his moral sense." There is something in this that rings true about Scott's first three solo albums. There was material on each of these offerings that may have shocked the listener's moral sense. Scott's rendition of Brel's "Next", with its references to a mobile army whorehouse, a queer lieutenant, and a dose of gonorrhoea stands out as a necessary shot at social hypocrisy, as do his covers of Brel's "Jackie", "The Girls And The Dogs", "Funeral Tango", "Amsterdam", and "My Death". British pop had resisted the inclusion of sexually explicit lyrics into its repertoire, and Scott's sympathies with the biting acerbity evident in Brel's writings led to him being thought of as one of the most controversial singers of his generation. The controversy surrounding the release of the censored "Jackie", as a single in 1967, had a lot to do with *Scott 2* going to the number one spot on its release in 1968. *Scott 2* was to feature testy lyrics in the form of Brel's "Jackie", "Next", the less suggestive "The Girls And The Dogs", and Scott's own composition, "The Girls From The Streets". The risqué lyrics were sanctioned by Scott's vocal authority, but the singer's temerity in endorsing material that was likely to shock, was a warning to record companies of Scott's singular artistic drive towards truth. Going against the grain of a career that should have established him as a standards singer, Scott's early rebellion suggested the later pitfalls he was to encounter. He would be progressively framed into a waiting silence by an industry suspicious of his unpredictable product. In his *Tilt* interviews, Scott will speak dejectedly of his failure to have projects financed over the years. How many ideas for potential Scott Walker records have been rejected?

It isn't that *Tilt* is unromantic. The deep-grained suffering evident on the record is lifted at times into transcendental longing. The sadness is tinged with romantic undertones, as when Scott sings, "Then higher above me", on "Farmer In The City", asserting the right to look up in hope, even when subjected to pain.

Does Scott I wonder, listen to Coil? Coil's song, "Ostia (The Death Of Pasolini)", on their *Horse Rotovator* album, covers a lyrical terrain not so dissimilar to Scott's "Farmer In The City". John Balance's lyrics for Coil's thematic homage to Pasolini are poetically evocative in their empathetic recreation of the director's murder. Balance's lyricism, skilfully employing half and full rhymes, extends to: "And his body rolls over/Crushed/from the shoulder/You can hear the/Bones humming/Singing like a puncture." There's an uncanny set of associations linking the two songs, Scott's allusions being the more enigmatic of the Pasolini homages; but both share in common a sense of redistributing their subject posthumously, through poetic resonance. Scott's "Farmer In The City", is "the journey of a life", as its flashbacks implode in consciousness, whereas Balance's approach for Coil's "Ostia", centres his subject in a more telescoped focus: "Throw his bones over/The White Cliffs/of Dover/And murder me/In Ostia." Coil have a rare poetic lyric-base to their highly idiosyncratic music, and there's a possibility that Scott has assimilated the daemon at the heart of their experimental oeuvre.

The relatively orthodox orchestral arrangements of "Farmer In The City", and "Patriot (A Single)", on *Tilt*, maintain Scott's spiritual commerce with the romantic aesthetic which so dominated his early choice of songs. But faced with the dissonant, percussive aspects of *Tilt*, which appear to owe something to industrial, Scott will say in his *NME* interview: "It's also a question of the recording. We wanted to record as naturally as possible, so we didn't use any compression. And so because *Tilt* is like a deep focus shot instead of a modern in-your-face noise, you really do have to play this record loud, because then it all comes together. Even when the bursts come in, like on 'The Cockfighter', you've gotta be brave and keep it loud."

Scott's explanation of *Tilt*'s sound-frame resembling "a deep focus shot", is also what imparts to some of the songs their distinctly filmic flavour. Whereas Scott's early songs were orchestrated with a Wagnerian density of sound, the arrangements on *Tilt* don't push the voice, rather they interpret it through suggestion. Scott is not being shouldered on the song's orchestral arc, as a die-hard romantic, but is content on *Tilt* to keep his romanticism low-key, and almost as it were, absorbed by the arrangements. But disguise it as he will, Scott's romantic wound bleeds into the context of *Tilt*, and there are moments of awesome intensity on the album, as in the nakedly vulnerable reading of "Rosary", when Scott's voice lifts out of the abyss to tremble on the most sensitive edges of being. The only way of getting there is through pain, but as in Dante's journey, the Inferno leads first of all to the intermediary Purgatoria, and finally to a visionary initiation to the Paradiso. Gary Leeds, the ex-Walker Brothers drummer, informed us on the Radio 2 Arts programme devoted to Scott, that the latter had told him that he expected never to record again after making *Tilt*, and that the album was the summation of his career. I suspect this reaction on Scott's part has to do with the anticlimactic aftermath of a period of intense creativity, rather than as serving as a final judgement on his voice.

Let's shift location in Scott's career to the title track from the regrouped Walker Brothers 1978 album *Nite Flights*. The song found its way on to David Bowie's 1993 album, *Black Tie White Noise*, where the vocal treatment is almost identical in pattern to Scott's much superior rendition of his own song. The Bowie version is manifestly a copy, and adds no interesting departure to Scott's neutrally delivered original. In fact, the neutral tone that Scott had hoped to provide for *Tilt* owes its origins to a much earlier period, and namely to the first of his trilogy of later albums. "Nite Flights" is the first delivered of Scott's wilfully recondite material. There's little cohesion to the lyrics, other than their embodying a sense of vertiginous panic, and the short lines in which words stand out like passengers' faces at departure gates, give emphasis to the sense of fear that generates the song. It's root terror that seems the genesis of lines like: "The dark dug up by dogs/the stitches torn and broke/the raw meat fist you choke/has hit the BLOODLITE." If the song owes its physiological origins to Scott's terror of flying, an aerophobic condition partly shared by Bowie, then its psychological thrust belongs to Scott's metaphysical hells. The curved melodic line on which the song progresses, suggests that it could have proved a hit single if it had been released in that format. Instead, both the song and the album after which it is named, were to serve as the blueprint for Scott's increasingly obscurer writing.

If "Nite Flights", as a song, was Scott's reaction to the chilling isolation and critical neglect he experienced as the seventies came to an end, then it couldn't have been more impenetrably measured. You can't get at the song to elucidate a meaning. The translucent vocal is completely at odds with the tortured lyric. It's this clash of oppositions which was to come to a head on *Climate Of Hunter*. "Nite Flights" touches on cut-up surreal, and one can understand Bowie's attraction to Scott's weird juxtaposition of imagery.

Nite Flights in terms of its sleeve design, is the first of Scott's

---

charcoal-grey trilogy. The sombre rain-sky tones which comprise its colouring are similarly repeated on *Climate Of Hunter*, and *Tilt*. The sleeves suggest a serious mental climate. They are not so much night skies as densely foggy days. It's only on the *Climate Of Hunter* sleeve, that Scott's recognisable features confront the camera, and correspondingly the purchaser. On *Nite Flights* his image is miniaturized and obscure, and on *Tilt*, he doesn't appear at all on the CD inlay. You have to open the accompanying booklet to find Scott in various permutations of image distortion. Three zinc-grey sleeves that correspond to something in Scott's representational psyche. I think *Tilt* should have carried a blueblack inlay to represent a journeying hope in a dark time.

Back to "Nite Flights". The song is glacial. It's about alienation. Its nerve hits the "BLOODLITE". The lyric chokes to strangulation, despite Scott's neutral vocal. It's about testing destiny to its ultimate frontier, and pushing the risk to an embraced suicide. Scott affirms, "we will be GODS on nite flights/with only one promise/only one way to FALL" – as though the high in avian ascent is matched by a corresponding fall.

Scott's romanticism often self-destructs in the need to take soundings in the experiential abyss. The material on *Nite Flights* crowds into a vacuum like cars into an underground tunnel. There's no way out. "Shutout" says precisely that. In a world in which the recognised apotheosis is "the GREAT DOLL", Scott sings of a climate in which "there is crouching and wailing on stones". The implications here are prophetic, as they are in the beyond-the-world extremes of experience recounted on *Climate Of Hunter* and *Tilt*. Part of Scott's dilemma must be, is there anyone really listening on the end of the line? People are hearing the consummate voice, but what about the lyrics? Is the voice posing a romantic lie? Does the vocal texture override the desperate arena of emotions that are nerve-ended into the lyrical content? *Nite Flights*, for which I believe his authorship to be uniform, is Scott's greatest nocturnal album. Its tension is unremitting, and there's no break in the circuit offered.

That's one kind of romanticism, and another is the Charles Aznavour cover, "Who (Will Take My Place)", from *Scott Sings Songs From His TV Series*. Charles Aznavour, as both a songwriter and melodic singer is central to French *chanson*. A bilingual performer, whose metaphysical themes echo Brel's preoccupations with love and death, Aznavour's songs have a rounder narrative feel, and are less angular in their cutting edge. Some of Aznavour's songs like "Yesterday When I Was Young", have been incorporated into the standards repertoire; and in 1993 Marc Almond was to cover the controversial, "What Makes A Man A Man", as a single with particular meaning to a gay ethos.

It's regrettable that Scott has never recorded the self-reflectively elegiac, "Yesterday When I Was Young", for one can imagine him pushing the song's potential to maximum poignancy. Scott's bluestreaked reading of "Who (Will Take My Place)", brings into melodic conflict the tensions between love and death. The song's protagonist speculates on the likelihood that his lover will find pleasure and consolation in other loves after his death. He has come to accept the premise that he will die, although regret permeates his feelings. Scott questions within the context of the song's reality: "Who will touch your face/Sleep in your embrace/Who will take my place/When I sleep alone." This particular theme of sexual jealousy is an unusual one for a song. Aznavour brings to life an emotional twist that we are all capable of entertaining. Scott handles the theme with the same seriousness that he brings to Brel's disturbing probes into psyche. The song is humanly dignified, for its protagonist is questioning himself rather than his love. The jealous motives are explicit: "Who will climb the heights/finding in your nights/all those wild delights/only I have known." I think of this song as exceptional in Scott's body of covers. The singing voice neither exaggerates nor understates the bitter reality of the proposition. There may have been more than a little autobiographical resonance to the song, for at the time of the recording it in 1969, Scott had formed a close relationship with the twenty-year-old, Mette Teglbjaerg, whom he had met in Copenhagen in June, 1966, and whom he was to marry in 1973, in a private ceremony at a chapel in Las Vegas, subsequent to the birth of their daughter Lee on 30 August, 1972. The distinctive Scott empathy that has him meet a song right at its emotional centre, is abundantly alive on this cover. Singers differ from poets in that they can vignette a whole aspect of themselves in a single vocal flourish. Feeling that has been buried deep is surfaced in a moment of spontaneous recognition. The poet's way is often a more cumulative build-up of subtle energies, so that the meaning is coaxed out of a complex of conscious and unconscious associations.

Aznavour's narrative structures are tightly framed, and Scott models his version accordingly. There are no mis-sightings in this story of telescoped grief. Compassion and regret symbiose in realisations like: "When I end my years/Who will ease your pain/Kiss away your tears/And bury me again."

Who?

Scott is still there on this London afternoon. It's actually a Thursday in February, and one that burns clear like a blue diamond. You can feel the cold collect in exposed areas of skin. Scott may be pushing the air on a bike travelling west towards Chiswick. Or he may be doing nothing until Friday. It's a matter of preference.

There are only two album sleeves on which Scott visibly appears in make-up. On both *The Moviegoer*, and its successor, *Any Day Now*, Scott can be seen with his eyes emphasised by black eye-liner. In the photograph used for *Any Day Now*, he is seen wearing a translucently porcelain foundation. The refined sensitivity of his face is enhanced by subtle make-up. He looks every bit like Rudolf Nureyev's counterpart in aesthetically delineated features. Scott, with a different orientation could have been the ambivalent icon to a seventies bisexual culture. The song "Big Louise" had more than hinted at Scott's sympathies with minorities.

There's something about Scott's relation to his work that has never come clear, largely I think because it lacks definition for the artist. Prior to Scott's late trilogy of albums, his music had always been without a defined focus. His first three solo albums released between 1967–69, created a homogeneity of contents, but they never described a commitment to a musical direction. The self-penned ballads, the standards, and the Brel covers which the albums comprised were sewn together by Scott's ability to have his voice meet with the solitary image of himself cultivated by his fan-base. But his first three albums were also outstanding for their limitations. The formula couldn't be endlessly repeated without diminishing effects. *Scott 3* ever so slightly diversifies the medium adopted, but offers no room for expansion. When Scott stepped out of the format, he devolved into the directionless chaos of *Scott 4*, and *Til The Band Comes In*, where his confusion has him experiment with all manner of unconvincing styles. He seemed in 1970 to have abdicated his voice, and to be scrambling to find a musical persona through which to reinvent himself. Looking back it seems an amazing phenomenon in itself that Scott's first three sombrely intense ballad albums were the commercial successes they proved. They could also have been the end of Scott Walker. Artists intersect with their felicitous moment in time, and Scott appeared to have foundered on the threshold to the seventies.

1970 was the crucial turning point in Scott's career. The American poet Robert Lowell, speaking of his transitional collection *Life Studies* (1959), once questioned whether the book had offered him a lifeline or a rope with which to hang himself. Scott's radical abandonment of ballad singing, at the end of 1969, for the eclectically based pop on *Scott 4*, was a move conducted without a natural gift for the contagious melody line on which pop hits are structured. None of Scott's major hits in the sixties was self-penned. The Walker Brothers rode high on Bacharach/David compositions, and Scott's solo hits, "Jackie", "Joanna", and "The Lights Of Cincinatti" were the products of others. Although songs like "The Seventh Seal", and "Angels Of Ashes", on *Scott 4*, are examples of Scott, the poetic lyricist, the overall feel of his first self-penned album is one of incomplete fragments. The album has the pervasive self-destructive feel for which it is so admired. The album's vocal mix finds Scott unusually and subversively casual in his delivery, and prepared to squander the perfect diction on which he had established a reputation. Not that the laziness is without seductive merit. Scott sounds so chillingly under-voiced on *Scott 4*, that the assumption is that he's either drunk or couldn't care less about the consequences.

The album's successor, *Til The Band Comes In*, deepens the artist's sense of chaos. The self-penned suite of songs which goes to make up half the album's contents, ranges from the burlesque, "Jean The Machine", to the isolatedly confessional, "Time Operator", to the miniature ballad, "Thanks For Chicago Mr. James". There's no clear focus to this conceptualised project. The notion of apocalyptic catastrophe is evident in songs like "The War Is Over", and in the unsettling track, "Til The Band Comes In", but Scott was a long way from achieving the intense eschatological scenario he was to devise by way of *Tilt*. The only song in the suite to hint at possible commercial potential, and which was in fact scheduled for release as a single, is "Thanks For Chicago Mr. James". The number contains the melodic blueprint of a big Walker ballad, only to be self-destructively cut short, as though Scott is unwilling to satisfy the listener's expectations of the song's building along a balladic trajectory. The song tantalises rather than fulfils, and in this respect is true to the album's melange of opportunistic fragments that constitute no more than the sketches of songs.

At the time of releasing *Scott 3*, the artist had complained, no matter the album's peaking at No. 3 in the charts, that, "The Establishment have been trying to tell me for as long as I can remember, that the public won't understand what the hell I'm talking about on record." He also considered that, "The melody lines were too long, and people were puzzled and got bored halfway through."

Scott 4, and *Til The Band Comes In*, may be considered as Scott's deliberate deromanticisation of his image. He had deconstructed the notion of himself as a stereotypical crooner, but he was still a long way from perfecting his new idiom. If the melody lines are shorter, and the musical texture less extravagantly orchestrated, then Scott doesn't sound quite comfortable with his transitional material.

There is of course a justifiable claim for Scott's two experimental albums comprising buried masterpieces. Both albums allowed him to polish his gift for writing character studies, that peculiar Scott propensity for evoking domestic scenes in the lives of the solitary or alienated. A song like "Joe", off *Til The Band Comes In*, finds Scott sympathetically addressing old age in a character who is dying, an usual theme at a time when pop music was consumed by a youth culture dynamic. Tenderness and compassion are the usual modalities that Scott brings to his character studies. Scott was big enough at twenty-seven to have extended his emotional insightings to the acceptance that old age and death are experiential realities, and not fictions applicable to other people. There's every reason to ask of a pop song that it presents the compressed constituents of a short story, and that in doing so it eliminates the gratuitous and prosaic. Scott wasn't to meet with this criterion until his later trilogy of albums, and in 1970 he was a sensitive miniaturist, a writer who could adopt a persona for an imaginary dialogue with a time-operator, or find a purchase on the life of a Russian spy in "Jean The Machine". In 1970, Scott had discovered the black hole in being, but he was still circling the edges. His anxiety was channelled into the making of character studies, or life studies, to use Robert Lowell's expression. The romantic in him still believed that his sufferings were lessened by their belonging to the collective. By the time Scott came to record *Tilt*, the sense of naked isolation in the writing had become total. The landladies, solitary neighbours, social misfits and ruined lovers who populated his early songs had been left behind, and in their place was a man using his creativity to confront final things. Rather like the onion, Scott has shed his successive skins over the years, and what we are hearing now is the bruised, but purifying isolationist.

In 1995, Scott will say: "I don't like writing or anything like that... but it's a challenge. You ask a lot of people and they'll say the same thing – you've gotta get it down. So it becomes a very masochistic thing." And so we ask, is the antipathy to writing, the reason for Scott's extended silences? Does the creative block exist in the reluctance to commit himself to the written word? If we see Scott as essentially contemplative, then silence will be his presumed creative state. The work taken out of silence can be interpreted as a demystification of a spiritual ideal. Scott's deep pact with the inner worlds is a part of his introspective orientation. The act of making public what was private, and outer what was inner is a necessary condition of creativity. Artists like Scott find the exchange of states disquieting, and may prefer to remain in secret dialogue with themselves. Crossing the frontier means going public. It took almost thirteen years between *Climate Of Hunter*, and *Tilt*, for Scott to make that passage.

I come back to the notion of Scott as the archetypal romantic, unwilling to tolerate the desublimation of his ideals. A person

---

Another Tear Falls

undergoing this process is most often transformed from an aesthete to an ascetic. The supreme example of this type is the French writer, J.K. Huysmans, the author of the bizarrely decadent novel *Against Nature*. Disillusioned with the overload of sensory experience, and exhausted by his pursuit of beauty, Huysmans retired to a Benedictine monastery in the attempt to find the spiritual realisation of his aesthetic aspirations. Scott's destiny has also been one of a journey towards truth, and he has renounced the prosperity of riches to live the relatively frugal life of someone preoccupied with inner concerns. In his song "Angels Of Ashes", from *Scott 4*, he consoles himself with the awareness that: "If you're down to an echo/They just might remember your name." The sense of an intermediary, or spiritual guardian being there in one's darkest hours is the companionable aspect that goes to make up this lyric. The song comprises a note of high beauty on *Scott 4*; and the feeling that angels transpose themselves from molecular holographs to manifestations of flame is part of Scott's apprehension of the angelic kingdoms.

Something of Scott's humility and disaffection from materialism, comes across in lines like: "With my one suit/badly pressed and worn/like a child left in the world alone" from "Such A Small Love" on *Scott*. There's a willingness on his part to let go of things, and to be. Scott's songs are very much about the onion process. They strip the exterior from things and aim for the truth at the centre. They are never about accumulation; they are invariably the subject of loss. The characters in Scott's songs aren't rich, and none of them aspires to a fantasy wealth. Their concerns like the singer's are with coming to terms with the big events like identity, self-truth, acceptance of psyche's contents, and ultimately with death.

The romantic image of Scott Walker will always stay. The Bob Carlos Clarke photograph on which I have remarked, finds Scott as a post-romantic. It catches him at the transitional age of forty, and as a serious artist bringing his life into conciliation with his work. I return to this photograph because I feel it's as close to Scott as we'll ever get. In real time the artist appears acutely and uncomfortably self-conscious. Clarke has caught Scott without shades, and in a manner in which the subject's inner story comes through. Scott is momentarily out of hiding. He is brought to the edge of visual confession. His silence speaks in the way that photographs have a vocabulary independent of their image-contents. Clarke has succeeded in removing Scott from the idea of being photographed. By this I mean Scott is in discourse with his natural self, and not in dialogue with the camera. In terms of voice, this is how we would imagine Scott to be in the studio. Slightly quizzed, creatively alert, and intensely preoccupied with inner affairs.

If you're a romantic, then you'll be time-framed into Scott's sixties work. We listen to Scott sing "Another Tear Falls", and arguably we would wish to be inside the song, for all of its blue, lachrymosal sadness. We would like to be experience the sadness in order to know the voice better. The whole song is a blue wash. We will experience it again on "Stay With Me Baby", and exit on the mood with "Walking In The Rain". "Another Tear Falls" was the last of the Walker Brothers' substantial hits, excepting the much later in time, "No Regrets". It's not a great Bacharach/David number, at least not lyrically, but Scott's voice makes it monumental. You listen to the vocal architectonics, and the voice seems to stay in the roof. It's one of the most bluely romantic renditions of a song ever delivered. And it's not studio time we're witnessing here, it's Scott's genuine inconsolability. It's to my mind the best of the songs with which the Walker Brothers indented the charts. The band were already slipping from favour, and Scott knows it, as he shapelifts the lyric into a blue cloud. Listening to the song occupies our complete attention. In the moment of hearing, the voice places you directly in the present. You're crowded out of any concern with the past or the future. "Another Tear Falls", offers no least fractional overlap.

It's a Wednesday that brings my fourth encounter with Scott to a close. It's still February, and the beginnings of purple crocuses point to the coming spring. It's not here yet, but it's a virtual presence. Wednesdays differ from Fridays in their median placing in the week. They're a middle day, like Scott's middle years. A time for evaluative reflection. Scott's probably sunk right into himself on Wednesdays. Wednesdays are the colour of "Such A Small Love", Thursdays of "Montague Terrace In Blue". The singer's voice is doubtless on hold; but the man's out doing. When he hears himself speak, it's without touching his creative core. Like at the supermarket, or the newsagents, or anywhere else where we are absolutely ordinary.

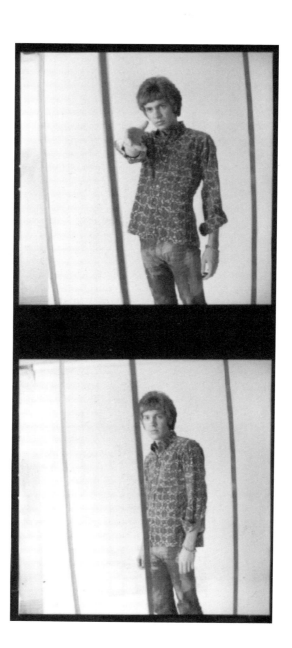

IF SHE WALKED INTO MY LIFE TODAY

There comes a time in a singer's or a writer's career, when the artist's name becomes a substitute for the work. We neither listen to, nor read the new product, rather we assign it to the general idea of the artist's oeuvre, and feel without exploring, that we are familiar with the contents.

But with Scott's minimal output over recent decades, the reverse is true. The release of any Scott Walker album is likely to be greeted with the critical curiosity attached to a major event. We ask ourselves by way of response, where do people go when they disappear, and do they come back from their missing time as the same person? Do they still profess the same enthusiasm for their art? The question most asked about Scott relates to the doing process. What does a committed artist do in twelve years' recording inactivity? He presumably doesn't concern himself with making records. In 1995, Scott will say: "I had a flirtation with 'Let Me Into Your Living Room, Folks' music, because people were winding me up about it, saying, 'You can be the next Sinatra'. But that's really boring unless you're going to really immerse yourself in it, because after all, those guys have been singing that stuff in nightclubs for years. I wouldn't even attempt to do that now... Unless someone winds me up, and I become a drug addict or something."

Scott must often reflect on the career possibilities that he extinguished. We all contain within us the fantasy of unlived potential, the apprehension of alternative existences through which we would have experienced life differently. If Scott had pursued the nightclub emporia, he would if things had proceeded propitiously have found the way to the chandeliered top of his profession. His name would have been constellated in the neon deserts. The antidote to this fantasy is to look at Scott's spiritual preoccupations as they are reflected in his latter trilogy of albums. They're certainly not as lyric

---

values compatible with a Las Vegas lifestyle. If, as I believe, the ways to knowing Scott are through his writing, then the inner territory he has explored is the reason for his rejecting stardom. Nightclub singers translate standards into entertainment. The singing's not about subjectivizing inner states, nor is it about the obscurity often associated with this process. On the contrary, it's about meeting the audience on a level with which they feel comfortable. The ups and downs of love and fortune are the usual subject matter employed by the singer.

Before I get to Scott's inner conflicts, I want to bring the cover "If She Walked Into My Life Today" into the arena of Scott's repertoire. Dismissed by Scott's biographers as an instance of ephemera, the song is nonetheless a near perfect rendition of an expression of self-questioning regret on the singer's part. Scott makes the song autobiographical. "I never really found the girl before I lost her," he sings, reflecting on his love, everyone's loves, and the insoluble enigmas within relationships that we only really address after we've lost love. Scott executes the song with none of the sense of generic ennui that Sinatra brings to his lowlight reveries. Sinatra's late-night tone confides, it is intimate and lived-in, it is unsurprised by its discoveries, and consummate in its acceptance of pain. Sinatra's voice doesn't so much neutralize suffering, as absorb it into a constituent of delivery. Sinatra is philosophic in his interpretations, whereas Scott's register is more one of committing his voice to realised anguish. Sinatra steps back from emotional conflict, tilts a fedora over his eyes, and muses on the impossibilities of love with an air of indifference. Sinatra's voice suggests the solutions to a remedy for heartache, namely to begin again with somebody else.

Scott doesn't bring that possibility to a song. His approach to covers is singular, in the way that in life we often become trapped within a set of emotional problems. The usual response to losing love is to be frightened that we will never find it again. It's this mode of address that colours nearly all of Scott's love songs. Scott makes the fear a reality in the cover under discussion, when he reflects on a list of catalogued shortcomings. "Did she mind the lonely nights/Did she count the empty days," he ponders, before expanding his omissions into behavioural ones: "Was I silent, was I cold/Was I too quick to scold/Was I too slow to praise." These are questions that most abandoned lovers ask themselves, but within the context of song the lyric is hugely magnified, and ordinary words depend on a feeling-tone to give them emotional charge. You have the notion with Scott that he chose the song because it mirrored an experience with which he was familiar. Scott's moody temperament, and the restlessness of his inner enquiries suggests that he is not suited to permanent relationships. His demand for private space has instated in him the need to be alone. Scott, who married Mette Teglbjaerg in 1972, and divorced her in 1975, is evidently best suited to a marriage with solitude. "I like sensitive people, but most of all I like girls who try to understand or at least listen with some sympathy," he had stated in 1965, at a time when his personal life was beleaguered by hysterical fans. Scott's version of "If She Walked Into My Life Today", seems to suggest that he was already at the time of recording the song in 1969, setting a distance between himself and love. The song isn't so much premonitory of the eventual collapse of his marriage, as a sighting about himself as someone who is probably consoled by the aftermath of love, and the relief that a relationship has come to an end. Scott's tone on this song is one of ambivalent regret. The girl has gone, but there's a bittersweet residue of relief attached to the loss. It's sometimes easier to experience unrequited love, or to engage in reflection on a relationship that never really worked. Scott's tone familiarises the latter two roles. His manner of colouring a song lends itself best to a theme of loss. Both Scott and his torchy counterpart, Marc Almond, possess voices grained with innate sadness, and neither is suited to the genre of light-hearted singing that most often passes for easy listening. Neither possesses a voice that can be backgrounded, or let float without attachment to lyrics. There are fine singing voices which don't necessarily rely on being foregrounded. You can take the tone on trust, and not pay vital attention to the lyrics. It's an art that nightclub singers often adopt to perfection. It's how they're singing, and not what they're singing, that counts. Your ear doesn't mind the missing pieces in the aural jigsaw puzzle. Scott's voice, like Almond's, is too intrusive, and too idiosyncratically charged to be neutered by a Las Vegas ballroom. I return to the fact that for Scott, the singular qualities of voice are both an advantage and a detriment. You either like the concentrated pitch, or it means nothing to you at all. It's not a tone that can be cocktailed into fusion or lost in the mix. It is a voice so staggeringly isolated as to appear one of a species, and utterly lonely as a consequence.

Scott's voice, so rarely now on show, but known deeply to the collective voice-consciousness has become a metaphor for a hibernative creature. The Scott-voice we listen to belongs to the past in the absence of present continuity. It's only in a live context that voice is ever situated direct in the present, for recording entails a time-lag. We hear the past recreated as the present. Scott is the digital time-traveller, who is always arriving somewhere.

I want to jump back in time, and cameo the near perfect "Rosemary", from *Scott 3*. As important a song as "Big Louise", in terms of character study, "Rosemary" is another of Scott's psychological vignettes to manifest a profound understanding of the feminine. "Rosemary", together with "It's Raining Today", and "Big Louise", defined the melancholy, rainy mood that predominates on *Scott 3*. It forms part of a triptych of songs that seem pretty much to crystallize Scott's emotional spectrum at the time. Rosemary lives in waiting and sad longing. I speak of her as a reality, for within the context of the song she steps out of fiction into assumed reality. Rosemary spends her time waiting for a travelling salesman, called Mr. Gin, to return from his travels. Her loneliness is windowed on emotional vacancy. She feels life hammer nails "in the coffin of her youth". Scott's songs in the late sixties are all about mourning the passing of time. His characters, like Rosemary, are powerless to reverse the situation, and their frustration at the prospects of growing older are expressed through sometimes desperate actions. Scott had said it all about himself in his self-composition "The Plague", a song that had served as the flip-side to his 1967 single, "Jackie".

The song "Rosemary", exemplifies the use of long melody lines, a characteristic Scott was to react against when he came to record *Scott 4*. I like the mid-song externalization of Rosemary's separation from life, when Scott turns his subject transparent: "Who are you and where you been/suspended in a weightless wind/watching trains go by from platforms in the rain." And isn't this what the song creates, the feeling of a character indefinitely suspended in life, and by her own measure vitrifying in solitude? Rosemary finds herself caught up in symbols that remind her of her lover's absence. She listens to boats journeying down the river, she stands on platforms watching trains pass through, and she finds herself somnambulistically walking across the floorboards under moonlight. What Scott captures in "Rosemary" are the isolated moments that we remember for ever, those indelibly painful realisations about life and love that leave inerasible fingerprints on memory. Scott was familiar with the experience before he wrote the song, but in the course of writing it his awareness deepened into self-discovery. Rosemary became an embodiment of himself, as well as an independently realised character.

There aren't many male songwriters who treat women as a theme with Scott's sensitivity. Scott's highly developed anima allows him to empathise with the feminine, and to understand the role that love plays in a woman's life. Something of Scott's own generic heartbreak finds its correspondence in "Rosemary". Within the song's parameters, Rosemary will always remain unfulfilled, in the way that Scott's creative aspirations will always fall short of his vision. The act of creativity is in a way an admission that we can aspire to, but never reach our intended state of self-realisation. Scott touches on that charge in his lifting cover, "The Impossible Dream", in which his voice points up from the abdomen on a vertical trajectory to the stars.

"Rosemary" is one of the abandoned ones who occupy Scott's songs. At the end of the number, he has her say: "That's what I want, a new shot at life/But my coat's too thin, my feet won't fly/And I watch the wind, and I see another dream blowing by." Rosemary's unfulfilment leads to her being trapped within illusion. We all know the sort of light-headedness that comes of challenging a big wind, and here it seems as though Rosemary's disorientating dream-world finds its parallel in wind. I do feel that when Scott left the studio after having cut this song, it wasn't as an artist who had executed a polished vocal, but as someone whose inner life was as troubled as the subject of his lyrics. Scott would have taken "Rosemary", and "Big Louise", back home with him as active components in psyche.

"Rosemary" is sung as an urgent directive to a sleepiness that has us hang on to bad relationships, rather than face the prospect of being alone. It's a different set of affairs to the active sadness expressed in "Joanna", where there's still the hope that love can be turned round in a positive way, and to the languorous regret expressed in "Through A Long And Sleepless Night". The latter song is late-night and soporific in the tone conveyed, and a rare example of Scott finding a relaxed pivot in a love song. His vocals surf the lyrics, as though the affair is now dulled in pain, and the nerve-tips are less alert to traumatic aftermath. But this cover, like "Joanna", is supported by the hope that love can still be retrieved. It's not an option open to "Rosemary", whose affair comprises nothing but transient sex followed by rejection. Neither "Joanna", nor "Through A Long And Sleepness Night", touches on Scott's indigo tonal spectrum. They both qualify as mid-blue excursions into heartbreak singing.

There's always a dual aspect to creativity. While the artist writes out of a desire to personalise experience, he is nonetheless conscious of needing to sight a public. Compromise is usually made in the interests of clarity, and at the expense of being too hermetic or subjectively obscure. In the writing of a song like "Rosemary", Scott has made the extension between private and public worlds, a bridge that he is not always willing to cross on *Climate Of Hunter*, and *Tilt*.

On the Interview CD for *Tilt*, Scott speaks of his singing voice as being the result of intuitive feeling, rather than the sound-product of voice coaching. He is typically unwilling to expand on the organic constituents of voice, for the latter comes naturally to him, and is therefore without the significance that it carries for the listener. In the mid-sixties, Scott was sent to be taught breath-control by the vocal tutor, Freddie Winrose, in his Denmark Street studio. At the time,

Scott acknowledged: "On a good day I've got a two and a half octave range which is pretty phenomenal. My biggest problem is my breath control. I guess I'm not healthy enough." Sent to Winrose, with the idea of eliminating vibrato from his voice, Scott would dutifully show up on days when he was due to record. In retrospect, he would say of Freddie Winrose: "He greatly increased my range, dexterity and confidence. But most important for me was his way of teaching breath control..."

We know that Sinatra would incorporate underwater swimming into his program of vocal training, so as to extend breath control when singing. Scott was taught a similar method of taking a breath, holding it, and then walking seven paces before its release. Sinatra has spoken of the method, with unnerving truth: "You've got to get up and sing, but still have enough down here to make your phrases much more understandable and elongated, so that the entire thought of the song is there." But Sinatra's incomparable inflections and nuances create a feeling of pivotal stability within a song, and so much so that it has been suggested that he invented the standard. You're not going to find him outside of essentially swing interpretations. Scott fits in here with the notion of conveying "the entire thought of the song". Like Sinatra, he doesn't chop phrases, and so the song's expressive motivation is seamless. Scott doesn't have the listener lose picture of the song's overall theme. Whether he is singing, "It's Raining Today", or "Farmer In The City", he is constantly present to the reality of the song. You feel the singer windowed in his phrasing, and with the song's thematic beginning and end constantly in focus. These same qualities are present in the writing of a good poem. There's a circular feel to the work, as though the images are looped. Sinatra's demands for "the entire thought of the song to be present", aren't so easily taken up, but are written into Scott's delivery.

While Sinatra has cited Billie Holiday as the foremost influence on his voice, Scott has never provided a specific indication as to a role-model. He has adopted the Judy Garland trademark, a trait also shared by Frank Sinatra, Tony Bennett, and Jack Jones, of having a ballad start out small and build by dramatic intensification. The song's climax suggests there is nowhere else to go, and that the trajectory blows apart at this point. It's the singer's way of self-destructing a cathartic dénouement. The time-frame has been blown. Repeat play is the only way of reliving the experience.

In later years, Scott has offered no clues as to his listening preferences. He tells us in his 1995 *NME* interview of having received records from nineties bands like the Tindersticks and Divine Comedy, but he offers no comment on the merits of his patently influenced protegés. With the exception of Marc Almond, the last two decades have been sterile in terms of generating male ballad singers of Scott's melodic genre, and so we suspect his listening comprises classical music, rather than pop. Scott is so adept at knowing the particular sound he wants, that he will in writing, compound all manner of diverse fusion into his perfected musical architecture. For Scott, singing is all about bringing a preconceived idea of sound into a studio reality. It's a more ingeniously sophisticated approach to a method, than Tony Bennett's one of enthusiastic immediacy: "I like to sing, as if I just picked up the lead sheet for the first time and the tune struck me."

Scott's refinement has of course grown in proportion to his songwriting abilities. He is no longer going in to the studio to read new life into standards, but rather attempting to give body to an infrastructural chrysalis of self-composition. A twelve-year germination carries with it a corresponding responsibility. *Tilt* is a record that comes out of a deep private space.

In a 1995 phone-interview published in the Danish journal, *Wild Magazine*, Scott commented on the inherent sadness at the heart of his work. Looking back to the time of his brief residence in Copenhagen, and to his love of the Danish philosopher, Soren Kierkegaard, he was to comment: "But it's true, I have always been influenced by the existentialists and their dualistic view on life. As you say, there was always, even in my most banal happy-go-lucky love songs, a strong touch of melancholy. That's also one of the things which made the role of pop star so difficult for me to adopt. Any kind of uniformity or formality in music or other things drives me crazy. I'm very uncomfortable with blocked or given situations."

The existential credo, via Jean-Paul Sartre and Albert Camus, and their predecessors like Kierkegaard, of man being responsible for his own freedom, is deeply written into Scott's life. We might call Scott an enduring existentialist, and an artist committed to a destiny which involves a long and solitary process of self-discovery. Scott's individual truth is not one that concerns itself with illusions. He is transparently aware that wealth and material items cannot shelter the individual from spiritual absolutes. Ever since the sixties, success in pop music has come to be associated with rampantly hedonistic lifestyles, and with the sort of plutocratic despotism reminiscent of the last Roman Emperors. Sex, drugs, and media adulation have become the outward manifestations of megastardom. It's not a world with which Scott is likely to sympathise. Of his new album, he will say: "I would like you to feel like you're in the middle of a heavy flu when you put on *Tilt*."

In the same Danish interview, Scott will say: "It is true that there are so many records today which just play on in 4/4 beat, and that limits your possibilities of opening people's imagination. It's the same with language. We have used it up in a way that no one today can bother listening to the content. I start out with very political statements, but try to lead the listener into a more open dimension by breaking the used-up words down and putting them back together again."

It's hard to imagine any other singer today commenting so intelligently on his work, or coming to it with such profound psychological insight. Scott's ability, not only in the writing, but also in the singing on *Tilt*, to turn the overtly political into the privately lyrical, is an act of real significance in the world of song. The achievement is of course dependent on precisely Scott's subtle up-ending of language, so that literal meanings are chased out in the interests of tonal texture.

Unless you're an unmodified hedonist, or a sex-addicted sensualist, people don't usually incorporate that much excitement into their lives. The problem with being a star is that people assume the individual lives an extraordinary life. And if like Scott you retain decades of impenetrable, silent mystique, then you are considered to be hiding some aberration from the world. In the interview given to *Wild Magazine*, Scott states: "It is true that I live by myself and spend most of my time painting, reading or biking around to my favourite pubs for a game of darts, but I also have a lot of friends and do not see myself as particularly weird."

When somebody is as removed from the public as Scott, in terms of direct accessibility, then all manner of rumours will find their way into circulation. There have been variously posted abroad the idea that Scott was working as a mini-cab driver, and that he was either mad or sectioned or dead. Rumours of the latter, which persist to this day, may owe their origins to 1974, when the financially pressurised John Maus formed a cabaret act called The New Walker Brothers. Jimmy Wilson, who acted as a surrogate Scott, on the band's cabaret circuit, died in a farming accident some years later, giving rise to the unpremised authority that Scott Walker is dead.

Rumours of a death, particularly when they relate to an artist who is believed to have a history of suicide attempts, go deep into the collective unconscious. Scott has died so often in his career, that the susceptible may assume the metaphor is a reality. We've experienced Scott's death, with the demise of the Walker Brothers in 1967, and again in 1978, and in various permutations of his solo career. The unnervingly extended silence between the release of *Climate Of Hunter*, and its successor, *Tilt*, was another form of death. At so many times in his career, Scott has been absent. Faced with the post-human phenomenon of recorded voice, the listener has been all too ready to assent to the notion of Scott Walker's death. We could even carry this as far as supposing that *Tilt* is a posthumous recording, and that the Scott clone who conducted interviews, and who appeared briefly on two television shows was a programmed stand-in.

Back to assumed reality. Scott will say of *Tilt*: "If I had sung the material true to my earlier records, all the lazy journalists would have said that I was crooning. And I deliberately wanted to avoid soul music. I have no time for copying genres. I wanted a European atmosphere. The whole album only took six weeks to record, and if it had taken longer, I would have lost the intensity that I wished to convey to the listener."

Scott brings back into focus here, his almost pathological fear of being grouped with the Sinatra generation of singers. He evidently resists the proposition of his being considered a standards singer at the expense of his innovative self-compositions. What he has done is to react so extremely to the idea of his being categorized as a crooner, as to distance himself at the opposite end of the spectrum. If there wasn't a Sinatra, then there wouldn't be a *Tilt*.

Tony Bennett once said that there was no good pop singer whose phrasing wasn't influenced by Louis Armstrong. "Most people don't realise," he affirmed, "that Louis Armstrong has taught practically every pop singer of the day how to phrase correctly. Without this basic phrasing one cannot be a good pop singer." Scott, who is without the husky tone associated with both Armstrong, and to a lesser degree, Bennett, is still within their register of phrasing, no matter how much his intonation may differ. Scott uses voice with more imagination than preceding generations of vocalists. His intonation imagines beyond the lyric-frame, and it's perhaps this characteristic which separates him most distinctly from his contemporaries. The songs on *Climate Of Hunter*, and *Tilt*, are more imagined than felt. The singing can remain neutral in tone, because Scott concentrates on visualising the lyric contents. This may also account for why *Tilt* sounds so radically disarming on a first listen. Scott is attempting to do on record, something that more recognisably belongs to novelistic designs, or to painting. In his Danish interview, he will say: "It is important to me to give meaning back to words, and I have started to discover that this is only possible by emphasising the anti-word, the pause, the silence. A bit like in art, where at the moment concept and installation art are trying to pull the over-used expressions out of their connections, to try and rebuild their meaning."

We could argue that Sinatra and Bennett, while they perfectly accommodate the entire thought of the song, rarely convince us of having taken it a stage further into imagination. Both standardise their material, by which I mean they are conscious in the act of recording of being heard by an invisible audience. Scott appears to have let this impediment go in his later work, and to have arrived somewhere a long way out on his own.

Some of Scott's most polished, early vocal performances appear on the Walker Brothers' second album, *Portrait*. *Portrait* provides a blueprint for the sort of cobaltishly moody song that Scott was to progressively claim for his own. Beginning with the intimately vulnerable "In My Room", Scott sets the tone for an album that oscillates between solo balladic cameos, and upbeat, melodic pop. The choice of material, decidedly over-serious for pop, and showcasing Scott's inherent melancholy on the slow numbers, side-stepped the big ballad feel of their commercial singles. *Portrait* was prophetic of the role that Scott would assume as a solo artist. We are also given an early taste of Scott's compassion for the old, in the unlikely choice of the cover "Old Folks", a song so angular to the fizzy gradient of sixties youth culture as to appear perverse. Other choices of material, like the leisurely standard, "Summertime", on which Scott's vocals bask, as though he's singing from the heart of a cotton field, slow the album to ponderously evocative pockets of anti-pop. *Portrait*, like its predecessor *Take It Easy With The Walker Brothers*, is much more of an American album in tone and feeling, than any of Scott's subsequent solo projects. In fact, Scott's assimilation of European culture was remarkably rapid, and between his arrival in London in 1965, and the release of *Scott*, in 1967, he managed to shift the culture-point in his psyche. By the time of *Scott 3* in 1969, he was thoroughly Europeanised, and the songs on this album owe their origins to Scott's assimilation of the major literary and musical traditions generated by that culture. Europe is undoubtedly Scott's spiritual home, and anybody listening to the Frenchified undertones to Scott's first three solo albums would be forgiven for feeling that there was no unhappy severance of the umbilical between Scott and his native America. The authority with which Scott comes to his adopted sources suggests a quickly selective sensibility, and one that intuitively recognizes how best to address his inner needs. Scott's quantum cultural leap between 1965, and 1967, showed him possessed of an intelligence that would deepen over the decades, and become in time the assemblage-instructor of *Tilt*.

To my mind the outstanding song on *Portrait* is the Leiber/Stoller composition "Where's The Girl". As an early example of Scott's sensitivity to the loss element in love songs, "Where's The Girl" is executed with the fineness of someone touching notes with filigree.

Scott gets the empty feelings attendant on being deserted, right into the song's chemistry. His economy of phrasing matched with dark mood intonations holds the song to the light like a troubled jewel full of turbulent undertow.

Scott, who used to spend a lot of time at his producer Johnny Franz's Hampstead house, co-wrote the melodic "I Can See It Now", on *Portrait*, as well as owning authorship to "Saturday's Child" from the same album. Both are lightweight Scott compositions, although the two songs are infused with Scott's characteristic pessimism about the outcome of love. They are try-outs in Scott's deepening awareness as a songwriter of the experiential abysses to be encountered in life. They are a long way from sombre achievements like "Archangel", and "Such A Small Love", but they are pointers to Scott's beginnings as a songwriter who has consistently addressed the obliquely painful sides of love in a personal and transpersonal context. Scott's early songs are sometimes written in the third person, so as to avoid direct identification with the material. These blue-hearted vignettes of melodic pop, don't as yet push boundaries, but are elegant exercises in how to organise minimal narrative content into an emotional core. By the time of the Walker Brothers' third album, *Images* (1967), Scott had expanded his narrational abilities sufficiently to structure complex material like "Orpheus", and "Experience", around his voice. "Orpheus" finds Scott in his novella-technique of incorporating personae into the parameters of pop melody. "Orpheus" may be seen as a companion piece to "Mrs. Murphy", from the *Solo Scott/Solo John* EP released late the previous year. Both songs commission a theme of adultery with a twist as sinister as a Nabokov story. In "Orpheus", Scott sings with poetic realisation: "I'll steal your dreams for my shiny gold chain/And you'll wake with your eyes full of rain/Finding I've disappeared." These are lines to hold back from the song and ponder into meaningful possibilities. They are the contents of Scott's unconscious mind at a particular time: circa 1967. In the Greek myth Orpheus descended into the underworld to retrieve his dead bride, Eurydice, and the success of the mission depended on his not looking round at the following shade until he had returned to life. Orpheus violated Hermes' instructions, and later on in his grief-mutated life became a musician renowned for his lyre playing. Scott's obliquely tangential theme ends with the portent of madness, or of going round the bend as a consequence of freaked relationships. Orpheus ended his life dismembered.

"Orpheus" was considered an obscure song at the time of its release on *Images*. In 1995, Scott will say: "Today the pop scene is much more open, and you do not need to take on all the idol-clichés to sell records – someone like Michael Stipe – manages fine without.

It's much easier now to be judged by your music rather than your image. There are generally much wider possibilities for playing with the pop format..."

It's not only Scott who has gained retrospective space on his youthful immersion in sixties stardom, it's pop music itself which has grown to establish more expansively eclectic dimensions. The indie scene has demi-godded the unorthodox at the expense of mainstream artists, allowing today for most splinter factions to receive a critical profile. A record like *Tilt* has of course benefited from increasing catholicity of critical tolerance. This bizarre masterpiece, although looked upon with suspicion by the *NME* for example, was nonetheless reviewed seriously by the paper, no matter the record's apparent disaffection from pop.

Where are we on a rainy March afternoon? Searching for Scott means I have to inhabit a parallel dimension. The sort of zone where extraterrestrials show in their weird intersections with time. Everything's prematurely in flower. The forsythia's hectic yellow statement is companioned by a loaded magnolia. April is crowding into March, and the London rain measures the fast proliferation of blossom. Scott is often seen in anoraks. It's a day for his ordinary biker's defence against the intrusive elements. It's a day to play songs of his like, "The Girl I Lost In The Rain".

Writing about a hero, who correspondingly remains a mystery, brings into play the conflicting emotions of both wanting to know my subject, and to respect his inveterate privacy. I feel the same about Lautréamont. I'm glad that no papers have come to light to disprove the legend he has become to the cultural underworld. If Scott was to write an autobiography, we would be appalled at the self-destructive demystification involved in such a project. We would resent the denarration of a contemporary myth. The media's attempts to externally sensationalise the individual's privacy, have created a world of the uniformly translated anti-hero. Scott has resisted invasion, and in doing so has made a legitimate stance for the artist developing within the precincts of a respectful silence. Public lives are like rooms stepped into so often that the carpets have grown treacherously footprinted. Something as individually masterpieced as *Tilt* is the product of solitary independence, and of a life conducted with the blinds down.

The end of a fifth encounter with the absent one. We all have somebody in our lives about whom we could question the fictional outcome of "If She Walked Into My Life Today". The narration is open to how we fantasise about the consequences of old love finding a spotlight in the present. We might open our arms in celebration, pretend we didn't properly recognize our former love, or perversely walk away. Scott sings of some of the possibilities open to the reflective and largely self-blaming lover. There are probably truths in the song which correspond to his own life. There are times when we are all ambivalent about our needs. We both want, and yet we don't. We open the door and close it at the same time. We ruin ourselves in the process, and never forget our indecisiveness. We come to swallow on ourselves in solitude. Scott gets the whole spectrum of emotions into the song. There are blue nights when we listen to it, and feel at an end. It has all been impossible. On other days, a sweetly tempered melancholy makes the future appear possible. It's like life itself, coloured by a singer's feeling-tones.

NO REGRETS

Scott's interpretation of Tom Rush's six minute elegiac summation of lost love, "No Regrets", is delivered with a cool not altogether characteristic of the singer. With the reformed Brothers signed to Dick Leahy's GTO label in 1975, and with Scott's song-writing abilities considered too obscure to accommodate a hit single, it was decided by Leahy that they should cover Rush's infectiously melodic, "No Regrets". The song is in fact an uninterrupted Scott solo, and one in which his voice chooses intimate reflection as the vehicle of expression. Lyrically the song isn't very much, which may account for Scott's restrained delivery. The song doesn't lend itself to imaginative interpretation.

Scott's own marriage was falling apart at the time of recording "No Regrets", but this doesn't seem to become an emotional issue in his singing voice. He plays a waiting game with the ballad, endlessly holding back the anticipated high moments, so that the listener is in the position of someone acknowledging thunder, but frustrated by lack of the impending storm. Scott seems unwilling to push the song too far, and this may have been in the interests of searching for the Top Five hit that the song was to become. Scott pitches the song sensitively, but without deep-immersion involvement. Without a hit single to his name for six years, and with as many failed albums in his undertow, Scott's tentative approach to "No Regrets", may have reflected something of his wariness in starting out all over again in an industry that was about to be tested by the lacerating anarchy of punk. By February, 1976 "No Regrets" had climbed to No. 5 in the U.K. charts, and for a brief interlude it seemed as though the Walker Brothers were about to become reacquainted with the success they had experienced a decade earlier. But sadly, the initial material on which to build hits was missing from their repertoire, and their follow-up single "Lines", despite Scott's grandiose heroic vocal, made no impression on the charts. "Lines" is given an archetypal Walker Brothers treatment, the arrangement detonating with percussion, and the voice carrying to ballistic climax. It was the old formula repeated to perfection, but the times had changed. Written by Jerry Fuller, "Lines" narrates the perils of cocaine addiction, and is arguably a richer lyric than "No Regrets", and one that extends Scott's voice to epic proportions.

For Scott, the whole period must have resembled an unconvincing time-warp. He had relocated himself in a pop ethos at a time when he seemed to have severed all ties with that medium. The lack of conviction in his execution of some of the material assembled on *No Regrets*, and *Lines*, is apparent in the lacklustre production, and in the understated approach he brings to the songs at hand. The fault would appear to be an absence of material that Scott could imagine into meaningful uplift. His tone on both albums is melodically reserved, as though he's without a blue dye in his voice to shape-lift the song to dense-textured tragedy. Whereas, in the sixties, Johnny Franz had provided a transcendental sound-scaffolding to Scott's treatment of singles, which were not overtly inspired in terms of lyrics, the rather ordinary songs that comprised most of the material on *No Regrets*, and *Lines*, were left sounding inferior to Scott's vocals. The sound-pretence that had screened the ordinary lyrics in Scott's earlier commercial phase had been stripped away to reveal sometimes pedestrian songs.

Scott in 1976, and Scott in 1998, the year in which I'm writing this book. Neither year has offered the public access to anything revealing about Scott's situation in life. People get ill at times, but we have never overheard Scott's particular set of illnesses. We do know that in the seventies he became obsessed with vitamin supplements, and took inordinate quantities of pills as a mirror of what he thought his system required. Any benefits from this would have been largely psychological. Scott may well have got on to the notion that heavy drinking destroys B and C vitamins, and may have been taking the latter to offset the ravages of whisky consumption.

What was the quality of sunlight like outside Air Studios, on the afternoons that Scott went in to record? It was a different light in 1976, to that which we encounter in 1998. The dissolution of the ozone layer has made our light dangerous. And how have Scott's moods changed over the intervening twenty years? His pain has deepened, and this book is about density of blue. A blue mood that goes on being mixed to the sky colour of a Swiss lake. Scott's face is imaged in that lake, rather in the way that we see him moodily encapsulated in an eye on the artwork for *Scott 3*.

After the failure of "Lines", as a single, Scott tried the Boz

Scaggs number "We're All Alone" as a follow-up attempt at a hit. Despite the pleasingly melodic vocals, Scott is again constrained by the essentially mundane lyrics. He tries hard to arrest an emotional pivot in a song based on sentiment. The result was a resounding commercial failure. There didn't really appear anywhere for Scott to go at the time. His solo career had foundered earlier in the decade, and the Walker Brothers reunion had predictably generated a brief curiosity interest, before nose-diving into oblivion.

Staging a comeback is a desperate measure. The publicity surrounding an artist's return quickly incites critical comparisons, and the later act is invariably considered inferior to its original counterpart. If ever Scott's career looked to be without a future, it was in 1976. Regrouping the Walker Brothers could have been seen as a covert admission that Scott had reached an impasse as a solo artist. Standing outside Air Studios in the incandescent summer of 1976, Scott probably felt as though he still hadn't been heard at his best. He must have experienced deep frustration at his inability at the time to realise his full creative potential. There was something missing, and the answer was clearly within.

With Scott kept on a retainer by his sympathetic record label, he was once again to disappear without trace in 1977, and was rumoured according to some sources to be washing dishes in a restaurant. But silence and anonymity are the catalysts to Scott's creativity, and in this blank year he was to regenerate his songwriting faculties with an unpredicted twist of genius. Considered passé by an industry alert to the anarchic anti-pop zeitgeist initiated by punk, and with his back catalogue still undiscovered by the likes of Brian Eno and David Bowie, Scott appeared to be headed for the void. His first four solo albums had long ago been deleted, and Scott's critics had retroed him as part of a now obsolete sixties generation. If ever Scott had been turned round to face the wrong way it was in 1977. Desperation seems to have retriggered his impetus to write, so too the realisation that he would otherwise succumb to artistic extinction.

As an older performer threatened by the holocaustal rage of punk, David Bowie had astutely sidestepped competition by coming up with the innovatively obscure *Low*, a record which obliquely reflected his inner crises as they were activated by liquor and drugs. The sombre studio disarrangements on *Low*, belonged to Brian Eno's genius for using the studio as an instrument, and despite the uncommerciality of the project, Bowie was at last able to have himself taken seriously by critics. He had for the first time created a music which existed independent of his visual image. The cut-up lyric technique that Bowie had employed on *Low*, and which showed him at considerable disadvantage to its originator, William Burroughs, had randomed words into meaningless associations. It's an art that Bowie has never perfected, but the ideas generated by the method and production of *Low* may well have pointed up possibilities for Scott to create the suite of songs which became *Nite Flights*.

If *Nite Flights* had been the album with which the Walker Brothers had relaunched their career, its angularity and cutting-edge could well have scored points. It's ironic that Scott should have arrived at this sound as an afterthought to commercial failure. At the time, *Night Flights* was to prove as commercially unsuccessful as Bowie's excursions into electronic experimentation. The time wasn't right, but Scott had succeeded in refiring his creative energies, and he would come to benefit later from those who were subsequently attracted to the dull glow that the album emitted.

Scott in 1978 had repaired the damage done by the idea that he was creatively extinct. He had performed a feat of black alchemy in coming up with one of the most desperate lyric albums ever to be written. What is so compellingly freaky about the songs on *Nite Flights* is their utterly serious and non-sensational themes. Scott was now 35 years old, which is young for a singer, but a dubious age for somebody attempting to orchestrate a re-start in the pop world. He was recently divorced, and despite his having started a brief relationship with Denise Simpson, then personal assistant to Dick Leahy at GTO, Scott had become almost unconditionally solitary. He was to place the lid on his obscurity by turning down an offer by David Bowie to produce a Scott solo album for GTO.

Scott's psychological behaviour at the time, suggests somebody perversely set against the grain of self-interest. In the light of rejection, we tend to go inwards in the attempt to enhance damaged self-belief. An offer of help is often construed as an act of condescension. Scott would have been at a disadvantage to Bowie's popularity. He would also have been suspicious about the whole notion of success derived from associations with the famous. In retrospect, Scott's decision seems to have been a wise one and his integrity to have remained untarnished. If Scott has missed out on fame, it is because his artistic devotion has followed an inner path, in the way that imaginative writers become a cult who future generations read.

London on a blowy Thursday in March. Writing outside a cafe, one sees so many faces. It's rather like watching street cinema. The book is a product of my particular moment as it enters into Scott's actual and conjectured biography. Somebody is buying some purple tulips complemented by yellow mimosa at a nearby flower-stall. For the time occupied in watching the purchaser, this book hangs in suspension. I've let go of the book, and correspondingly of my connection to Scott. Both are momentarily out of the picture as my visual frame becomes preoccupied with an ordinary happening in reality. It occurs to me that the break in continuity is like a black-out. If I was to walk away from this book now, it would be left in a state of terminal incompletion. Scott would be virtualized in my posthumous inactivity.

What were Scott's regrets in 1978? Everything and nothing. What are his regrets in 1998? Nothing and everything. There are things about our lives that never change. They are just there like the sky.

Speaking to Richard Cook in 1984, Scott will say: "The idea is to make it resonate. If you can find a polemic there, good for you. But it's to get this resonating factor going. I don't cut up. I'm not that kind of writer... I have to work at it..." Scott is referring here to *Climate Of Hunter*, and the fact that the material needs to resonate with the listener's inner rhythm. With the increasing complexity of pop music, artists have found it necessary to legislate over their new material, and to offer exegeses as to their creative intentions. Scott's comments invariably point to his inner expression. He speaks in terms of diagrammatic places on a psychic map. It's not always an easy journey for the listener to locate himself in Scott's terrain. His later work is like a Kafka narrative. You arrive at the familiar to experience total alienation.

Saturday afternoons interface Sunday blues. People step off the working week dazed. Whatever energy resources remain to them are only in partial play. Individual freedom – Scott has it – is a priceless thing. Some people have no idea of how it is found, or what to do with it should it become an option. It can't be bought, and it is the clear light which makes life purposeful. Whatever the problems attendant on being a cult artist, Scott has placed freedom above compromise. It is the hardest won and most valuable of human attributes.

We know from Scott's admission that he hired a workman's cottage in Tunbridge Wells as a solitary and estranging base from which to work on *Climate Of Hunter*. Emerging from still another demotivated period Scott seems to have found himself intent on deconstructing the pop module on which the album is based, and reintegrating the fragments as constructive damage. When the album failed to mirror its worth in the charts, Scott would claim that the whole thing was nothing more than a send-up on his part.

Scott is abstruse in realising that no matter what changes he makes in his music, he will always be considered a pop singer. Because his voice has grown to be public property, and because the origins to his commercial fame belong to his achievements with the Walker Brothers, he can never in a way escape his prototypical roots. In his 1984, *NME* interview, he will say: "The problem I have is this basis as a pop musician, which is something you can never drop. You can use other disciplines, if you know how, but it's all according to the thing you do originally – everything will work around that. I could have done this whole album with just a bass tracked a few times, varispeeding it, and used some percussion."

Because a voice can be put on the airwaves at any time, and usually without reference to the date of the recording, and without indication of the singer's present work, there will be listeners ignorant of the mutations that Scott's career has undergone over the years. They will be introduced to a Scott held in suspension, and one whose creative state represents apparent discontinuity. Scott's deepest frustration is not one of lack of audience, but one of being translated back into a sixties modality. The situation is amplified by Scott's awareness of the problem, and his protracted silences may represent an unconscious prompting to dissociate from past identities, and to reinvent himself through an expression that appears to have no common identity with his publicly identifiable work. I could put it another way. Because Scott has the ultimate voice, and one which he could adapt to a number of mediums, he has chosen to silence it. In the same way, people who have too much often commit suicide, for the boundaries open to them may appear too infinitely expansive. Death under these circumstances may entail finding a singular focus, as opposed to a wide-screened confusion of possibilities. We all have our own way of getting there.

To consider Scott's silences negative is to disallow for the time needed in which to change. If his later albums had been orchestrated rise and fall ballads reminiscent of his late sixties work, then there would be reason to consider his creative vacuum negative. We would concede to Scott's having wasted time. But because he has out-distanced any apprehension of what his admirers may have predicted for his ongoing evolution as a musician, then his periods of inactivity should be seen as a necessary part of the process. At the time of *Climate Of Hunter*'s release in 1984, he will say: "I have a totally different record I want to do now, because I discovered all the new things I can use in the studio. But I have to wait. This is a waiting game." The waiting game was to go on for a decade, and the measured work to arrive as the excruciatingly vulnerable *Tilt*.

Scott is not the sort of artist to make public his differences with record companies, but in 1984, he will astonish us by professing the opposition he encountered in making his initial solo albums. He will say: "I can't tell you what a fight it was to make those first records, even though they were charting. It was like those people at Philips were just waiting to say, no more of this shit..."

Another time jump. From 1984 to 1967. Scott aficionados will know that the sessions for his first solo album generated three superb out-takes: "Free Again", "I Get Along Without You", and "I Think I'm Gettin' Over You". It is tragic that these three songs have never been incorporated into Scott compilations, for their vocal merits and characteristically ethereal orchestration make them equal to anything he recorded at the time. "Free Again" is an ultramarine-toned ballad, one in which Scott's voice is ponderously abyssal, as though he is singing to somebody who can hear him perfectly at the bottom of a ravine. The voice embodies a depth and emotional strength rare even for Scott, and "Free Again" employs a simple lyric narrating: "Free again/Back to being free again/Back to being me again", as the singer narrates the paradoxical theme of being free at the end of a love affair. We have all experienced the sometimes transient rush of euphoria that accompanies the death of love, only to find that we will of course never be free of memories. Scott's voice companions the dualistic undertones of a reflective ballad in which loss is celebrated as freedom. The two energies braid into one, as his voice lifts on the strings to impart an inimitable sense of dramatic hubris to the song's contents. "Free Again" is representative of Scott in his torch singer's role, a mode of singing he was to adopt in the years 1967–69. Scott sounded a natural born torch singer on his first two albums, and the reasons behind his adverse reaction to finding himself in a generically feminine role have never been established. Something in Scott resisted carrying it through, and he elected instead to present his solo artistry to a pop-tinged cabaret circuit in the North of England. Perhaps torch-singing demanded of him too close an identity with subjectivized material, and was therefore a threat to the singer's insulated sense of privacy. "Free Again" is one of Scott's torchiest renditions, and is qualitatively close to Shirley Bassey's histrionic manner of imparting dynamized emotion to big ballads.

The second out-take under consideration is "I Get Along Without You", an elegiac standard given idiosyncratic readings by all the greats, including Billie Holiday, who coming in behind the beat, slows the song down to late-night, rainy reverie. Scott's interpretation is torchier than any of its counterparts. He keeps the thought of the song slow, and its reach universal, but his extended melody lines impart extraordinary style to a song in which the theme is once again the unsettling well-being that a lover may feel in looking back over a past relationship. Scott fingerprints the lyrics with dramatic authority, and demonstrates his mastery of breath control, something he will casually refer to in 1984, as acquired from reading books on the subject. In the same radio interview with Tony Myatt, he will tell us that he had to pick up the technical rudiments of singing as best he could in 1964, as prior to taking the lead vocal on the Walker Brothers' first hit, "Love Her", he had considered himself a musician.

"I Get Along Without You" is in Scott's vocabulary a deep-water mood song, if you like them that way. It's hard with an artist who dissociates so totally from his earlier work to gain any clear sense of what a particular song meant to him at the time of recording it, other than a sense of perfecting the vocal. If Scott was to call his first solo album "my obsession", then we assume the material recorded communicated with him on a deep level. We imagine it occupied all of him in its execution. The difficulty belongs to the sense of self-disparagement with which the artist comes to judge his work. The infrequency of interviews further accentuates the distance Scott brings to his past, together with his adoption of a manner deliberately making casual of work committed to a serious vision. His laid-back interview style, deceptively and disarmingly off-centred, and intuitively screening personal reference, disallows the past an existence except on his terms. It seems impossible that so feeling an artist would lack even an amputee's shadow-pain for work from which he is disconnected, and so one attributes the motive of disinterest to his attitude. A disinterest tempered perhaps by the withheld conviction that the work deserved better in its reception.

The third of the 1967 out-takes, "I Think I'm Gettin' Over You", is to my mind the least convincing of the three ballads. The song carries an admixture of country in its arrangement, and the restricted melody line resists Scott's pushing the song on dramatic build. The three excluded songs from the *Scott* sessions are all chaptered into the common theme of psyche being expansively regenerated after it is liberated from dead love. The love songs on *Scott*, namely "The Big Hurt", "Always Coming Back To You", "When Joanna Loved Me", and "Through A Long Sleepless Night", are no more and no less personally revealing than the excluded material, and so there is no reason to consider that Scott was intent on concealing a vulnerably personalised wound.

Scott's former manager Ady Semel once spoke of a vast cache of unreleased Scott studio material that will probably never find release. There would have been out-takes from all of Scott's studio sessions, for the vinyl LP accommodated a playing time considerably less than the CD. Selective exclusion of material would have been standard protocol. We have to think of these tapes in terms of the imaginary Scott Walker. The material has entered missing time. It is associated with disinformation, or dead affairs.

Asked about the importance of recognition for his work, Scott will say in 1984: "It's a cliché, but in the end you have to work for yourself. It's come to me like that... That is the only way I can do it now, the only way I can make records."

Inwardly, it was probably no different for Scott in 1967. One suspects that his record buying public in the sixties were somewhat removed from the product they were actually purchasing. The name Scott Walker, and the complementary image was the commodity that sold.

A settled, pink, end of the afternoon sky in March. A wider frame would reveal an eruptively orange sunset, but in Soho it's hard to achieve an over-the-rooftops take on wide-screened sky. If you search through the Berwick Street secondhand record racks, you may discover some of the vintage Scott reissues and compilations on vinyl. The double album, *Spotlight On Scott Walker*, with sensitive liner notes written by Fred Dellar, is one to have, as is the companion volume, *Spotlight On The Walker Brothers*. The Scott solo double in its attractive royal blue sleeve is an uncommonly discerning selection of songs, and one which includes the otherwise unanthologised single, "I Still See You". You may find miscellaneous *Best Of*s, *This Is Scott Walker*, and various Philips cut-price selections of Scott's work, released in the sixties and seventies. These are identifiable vestiges of Scott's career, although one suspects he took no interest in their release. And throughout the time period in which these anthologies were issued, Scott appears frozen into the immutable selection of uninspired studio shots endlessly reformulated as picture sleeves. The albums form part of the acquisitive memorabilia valued by completists. They are not to be found in Scott's apartment. They are also associated with dead time. When we try to relate to the past, it involves an act of trust. Memory is the only verifiable witness to retrieving past events. As we grow older, we sometimes find ourselves rebuying things that we let go in youth. Like records. The dark has dropped now. Soho is logged to an unmanageable gridwork of intractable early-evening traffic.

I return to the phenomenon of time, and our inhabiting it with a psychophysical body. We are essentially walk-ins who are not here to stay. We make purposeful tracks, and then we're gone. The awareness of time is part of the oppositional tension at the heart of creativity. Scott's electing to pull the plug on time in terms of meeting its challenge with creative output, may be a voluntary or involuntary decision. An accountable hypothesis for Scott's disappearing acts may be one that considers the artist to be made dysfunctional through clinical depression. If Scott is the victim of the paralysing syndrome of pathological depression, then the zapping symptoms would account for his long periods of unexplained inactivity. Heavy drinking is often an attempted antidote to depression, a self-regulated means of trying to get above the illness' flattening effects. An absence of motivation and a lack of self-belief are only two of the counter-productively pernicious symptoms that the sufferer encounters. Both are detrimental to continuity considered as self-expression, and both seem to feature strongly in Scott's psychological behaviour. Scott's thermostat is probably set at moderate depression. Artists who have cyclothymic personalities, and who experience alternating highs and lows without causing a rupture in everyday functioning, are usually able to accommodate their mood swings to the inconsistencies of life. In fact, mood abnormalities are written into the creative sensibility; but should the oscillation between up and down prove extreme, then either could be inhibitive to the discipline needed in which to create. Major affective disorder may be a constituent of Scott's psychology, and would perhaps account for the repeat pattern of enthusiasm followed by dejection, that he has manifested both before and after the respective releases of *Climate Of Hunter*, and *Tilt*. Immediately subsequent to the release of both albums, he has expressed a purposeful desire to go back to the studio, and to record new projects. On neither occasion has the aspiration been realised, and this in turn may suggest that Scott reverts to a depressed state once the excitement surrounding release has abated.

I'm advancing little more than a theory, and applying it to the insoluble mystery of Scott's almost permanent absence from recording. None of his attempts to explain away the missing years has ever sounded plausible. The man is too intelligently curious and culturally refined for us to believe that he spends the years watching people play darts in London pubs. In his 1984 *NME* interview, and accounting then for a six years absence from recording, Scott will say: "Well, time flies when you're not working. I haven't been doing anything that anyone else wouldn't be doing. Movies, reading, music, everything... some travelling, but nothing exotic like I used to." Over the years, there has never been an independent commentator on Scott's activities. Nobody who has been close to him has ever offered a confessional word about the artist's private life. We feel from the largely objective opinions of his ex-colleagues, collected by Scott's biographers, Watkinson and Anderson, that none of them has attempted to insight Scott's inner world, that rich territory out of which he creates. We are given a skeletal picture of Scott's external activities at the height of his career, and meaningful vignettes of his studio professionalism, but none of the people interviewed for the book tells us anything profound about the psychological disposition of their subject. We are offered anecdotes in the place of truths.

We could conclude from this that Scott in his lifetime will

always prove the subject of fiction, rather than biography, and that he will remain outside public information. I could rephrase the issue, and ask, what is it that we wish to know about Scott? What is it that a biography attempts to provide? As a species we are inveterately curious about what constitutes creative genius. Because we can't reduce that faculty to neuro-psychological origins, the impulse continues to represent largely unanalysable subjective qualities. Creativity implies an irrepressible individual freedom. Those who have it shine. They set up a field of fascination to the would-bes that can prove dangerous. Biographies of artists can be seen as valuable attempts to provide a human framework to creative achievement. They humanise their subjects. It helps us to know that ordinariness is a part of all beings. We all, including Scott, visit supermarkets, off-licenses, cinemas, laundrettes, post offices etc. Some personalities resist biography: I suspect I'm talking of Scott. Nobody knows with more authority, how to sing: "This is how you disappear."

There are aspects of Scott's seeming indifference to the infra-structure of his work, which may in part be explained by eccentricity. Reminded of Anthony Braxton's omissions of titles to his work, Scott will say of the blanks on *Climate Of Hunter.* "For me it was just that the lyric was complete, and adding something later on was totally unnecessary. I didn't know it had been done before." Scott rightly points out that Braxton is an instrumentalist, whereas for a singer to work without titles is a move calculated to assassinate commercial appeal. The title of a song or a poem instates pivotal reference in the listener or reader, and establishes a specific idea on which the material depends. In songwriting, the title is invariably reflected in the hook, and the listener stores the song on this incentive. By stripping the signposting away from four of the eight songs on *Climate Of Hunter*, and by calling the single, "Track Three", Scott was complicitous in marginalising his already minimally postmodern material. Scott's apparent disengagement from commercial guidelines reads like risk tempered with maverick eccentricity. "Track Three" could be considered as the first truly melodic pop single to employ film technique in its lyric frame. "Track Three" also begs the question as to whether we ever truly listen to lyric content as it occurs on singles. We have become so used to background noise by way of uninspired lyrics, and to keyboard programming by way of accompaniment, that we may have let the idea of meaningfully poetic lyrics go. In recent years Marc Almond has struggled to maintain the role of the emotional singer as purveyor of poetic lyric at a time of its relative absence from the pop genre.

Scott's ideas, as they are presented in published interview form, are largely delivered in splinter sentences. Asked about how he imparts body to a song, Scott will say in 1984: "It's all down to taste, isn't it? You can hit a sequence of things in a song that will somehow match up and work. That's part of the magic. But it's a hard question." Allusions typify Scott's manner of addressing a subject, so that the matter in question is left partially opaque, and the highlights never fully followed through. Scott starts an answer, and then short-circuits on its development.

The end of our sixth encounter with the absent singer. It's once again a Friday, only it's a different Friday to the ones that concluded earlier chapters. Time has moved on. Neither I, Scott, nor the reader is the same person. We've all grown fractionally older and correspondingly deeper into experience. The process could be likened to taking to water. What we are all looking out for is inspiration, or the sudden moment that transforms us and everything out there. It's then that we feel most alive. Scott may or may not have found that state today. He may have begun, added to, or destroyed a work, or perhaps he couldn't care less on his way to the cinema. Lightning can strike anywhere. Time stands still when we're inspired. Consciousness then, wants nothing external to its focus. The moment is all inclusive, like the experience of listening to Scott's voice on a dark blue Friday. The voice fills everything, because it can never come that way again. It's for the time of delivery an absolute.

Time to make a break for the next chapter. I'm finishing this one in a café in Holland Park Avenue. A monolithic cloud tilts into a blue space. I watch it settle. In an hour it will rain.

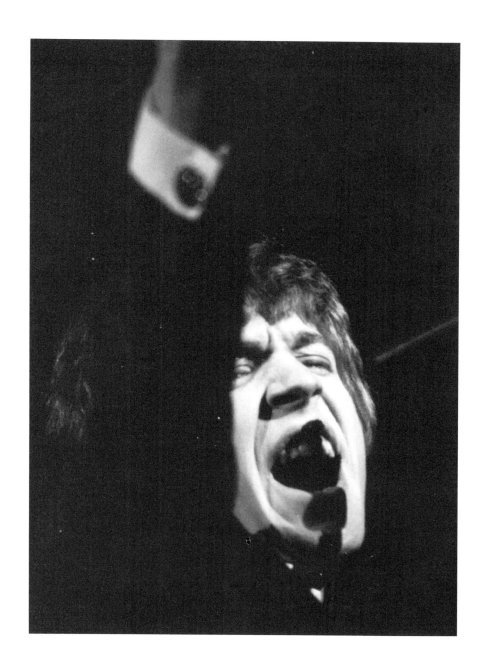

"LOOK UP, YOU COULD ALMOST SHRED THE STARS"

Right from the beginnings of his career with the Walker Brothers, Scott had expressed a profound dissatisfaction with the pop ethos as a meaningful vehicle for his art. There was an early sense of embarrassment on his part at the excessive adulation attached to pop stars, and the comparatively lightweight songs on which such fame rested. As an individual preoccupied with the search for inner truths, Scott was unlikely to be impressed by the criteria necessary to establish his continuity as a star. His sensibility recoiled from a popularity generated by a teenage fan-base. Unable to go out in public, and hunted from the car to the stage-door, Scott's privacy was torn at the seam, as the Walker Brothers rode high on their mid-sixties success.

For someone as innately introspective as Scott, stardom would have carried deeply traumatic consequences. It was as though the reflective window in which he lived had been broken, but not on the mystery for which he was searching, but rather on a public arena in which he found himself blindingly exposed. Scott was undoubtedly taken up by the excitement of it for a short time, but was quickly disillusioned by the constrictive pop format in which he found himself cast. He was unable and unwilling to act out the role of icon to an image-fixated audience. Scott transparently lacked security in himself, and therefore found it impossible to present the serene state of felicity necessary to convince an audience that he was enjoying the experience. Scott appeared to be evaluating his dissociation from the act in which he was participating, rather than proposing a future for the Walker Brothers. He seemed not to want to be there. This visible sense of bilocation in Scott's relation to himself, and his career, is a characteristic that has persisted throughout the decades.

It comes down to an essential lack of commitment on the

artist's part. How can a man so extravagantly talented use the creative expression of his being so infrequently? The fact that Scott never really intended to be a singer, may be a part of the problem. He clearly doesn't value his voice as an instrument he wishes to hear. Lack of self-esteem has him dismiss his work, and with it any sense of achieved continuity. In a very real sense, Scott has never committed himself to the role of singer. His brief flirtation with an effortlessly facilitated pop success reportedly resulted in a number of suicide attempts, and in a controlled but dependent alcoholism, while the metamorphic phases of his solo career have invited an inconsistent comparison to genius won at the expense of a bitterly endured solitude. Scott's career has found no even trajectory on which to build. His own lack of commitment to his voice has been central to his suspended motivation. Perhaps he has never seriously reflected on how his voice is missed. When we are low in ourselves, the idea of external interest in our art disappears. We can't in this state adopt the belief that an objective reading of the work may radically differ from the subjective impasse in which we find ourselves. The mirror into which we look is often too clouded to offer that option. We become sunk in ourselves like a shipwreck grounded in psyche. I imagine Scott spends a lot of time contemplating this wreck.

Because events happen so fast, we can spend a lifetime in a state of non-committal to the prominent aspect of ourselves. Scott seems to periodically turn back to a gift about which he is unsure, and an expression with which he has never fully engaged himself. Scott's sporadic returns as the man who has gone missing could almost be the subject of a story by Edgar Allan Poe. He comes back to spend a number of weeks in the studio, and to give several enigmatic interviews, before reoccupying a resolutely guarded private space. At the time of these happenings, there is both too much and too little conviction evinced by the artist. The seriousness he brings to the work is one of absolute, focused conviction, so that the listener starts to believe all over again in Scott's frustrated genius finding a means of self-expression, only to be let down by the artist's failure to build on momentum. From various hints that Scott lets drop in interviews, he seems very well informed of his past work, and yet he will profess no durable attachment to its contents. He will remind us that the Methodist Central Hall organ used on *Tilt* is a supercession of the church organ sound incorporated into the musical texture of "Archangel", but he will allow for no interest in the earlier experiment. His sense of commitment, or lack of it, will not extend to his establishing a holistic overview of his career as an artist and singer.

We could ask the question, to what is Scott committed, if anything, in terms of creative self-fulfilment. If he is only occasionally recalled to being a singer, then presumably his energies are permanently concentrated on something else. This something else need not be an art, but it obviously compensates for the absence of voice. Scott has spent less than six months in the past twenty years, in a recording studio. Does Scott fantasise about making films? As an enthusiastic cineaste, he must possess an encyclopaedic knowledge of cult films, and as so much of his later work relies on an image assemblage analogous to film technique, we assume that Scott would at times imagine himself in the process of making films. Scott was at one time rumoured to have become a Tibetan monk, but I suspect that during the time the rumour was in circulation, he was simply locked away in urban reclusion.

The truth of the matter is that our lives don't draw much attention to themselves outside our immediate circle of friends. Scott's biographers have related how when Scott's former record company needed to get in touch with him about the reissue of his Brel material, all contact had to be made through an intermediary, a friend of the singer, who in turn would act as a mediator to negotiations. Something of Scott's disconnection from events involving his career is manifested in this vignette depicting his disengagement from practical affairs. I suspect that Scott wouldn't be the sort of person to answer letters, or to situate himself in any imposed time-frame.

I began this chapter with the thought of commitment, and its context in relation to Scott's life as an artist. Detachment from one's art, or the cultivation of an air of disrespect for it, is written into certain creative sensibilities. Arthur Rimbaud, one of the visionary poets who have come to change the nature of how we perceive the world, expressed nothing but obscene disparagement for a gift he silenced at the age of nineteen. Baudelaire, systematically self-destructed himself and his poetic talent, Jean Genet despised literature, Billie Holiday expressed no joy in her art, Francis Bacon painted as an antidote to being permanently drunk, and Scott seems to belong to the same creative genome. He has never expressed deep anxiety over his lack of output, although he has called his inertia "shameful". Nor does he seem intent on making up for lost time. There has been no urgency on his part to remind the public of the extraordinary qualities he brings to voice. The problems of isolation, self-doubt, and the obscurity of the material he was in the process of writing would have contributed to his post-*Climate Of Hunter* silence, but the voice has returned to us in the form of *Tilt*, and there is every reason to hope that Scott will build on his masterpiece.

In 1993, and prior to recording *Tilt*, Scott put out an obscure single in France: "Man From Reno/Indecent Sacrifice". Scott contributed the lyrics to the two songs, and the music was written by Goran Bregovic, and both songs form part of the soundtrack for a film called *Toxic Affair*. The almost hermetic obscurity of this release – it was after all, the first time Scott had entered the studio for a decade – was matched by Scott's romantically melancholic reading of poetically infused lyrics. Both songs are invaluable, for they bond neither with Scott's past, nor his future work. They are weirdly isolated in timelessness. Again, the word posthumous comes to mind. Scott's voice, which is mixed here deeper than it is on *Tilt*, is nakedly alive to nuance-inflection, and grave in its evocation of disturbed lyric.

"Man From Reno" is the precursor to Scott's "Farmer In The City". It employs the same melody lines, only the place names are different, but breaks into a chorus introducing an occultized "Zodiac Killer". The addition of Mark Knopfler's melodically distinctive guitar on both songs creates a textural uplift that is sometimes missing on *Tilt*. Both songs are favoured by an originality that begs comparison, and by Scott's disembodied and displaced vocal readings. And isn't this one of the significant aspects that Scott has contributed to singing: the idea of nomadic voice? Scott's voice on "Man From Reno", and again on *Tilt*, finds a truly wastelanded tone, and at times sounds like an intermediary spirit caught between life and death. There is no earthed base to his timbre. In listening, we follow him out on an arc to nowhere. You don't arrive at a given place in pursuit of Scott's voice, rather you find yourself oddly reassured by the lack of signs on the way. Scott's is the voice that leads the listener towards an uncertain and always unresolved future.

The irrepressible romanticism in Scott resurfaces on "Man From Reno", in the form of his singing, "Look up you could almost shred the stars/Look up you might even stop the stars", as though the singer in addressing his despair, remembers the beauty of the star-filled heavens. Moments of spiritual reassurance occur similarly on *Tilt*, when Scott reaches for momentary lights in darkness. The song's sinisterly contrived subtext occurs in the chorus, when Scott sings: "Zodiac killers drain their hands/And wipe away the shadows from the walls/Neighbours all say he's got no friends/His friends all say you've got him by the balls." In a variant chorus, the crack that first appeared in Scott's song, "The Plague", returns in a similar context: "Zodiac Killer needs that crack/He wants you back/He's waiting in the bars."

"Indecent Sacrifice" concerns itself with a similarly obscure journey into light and dark as they occur in psyche, and as they register in experience. In this song the signposts are more obscurely juxtaposed, and the voice pitched deep into the journeying night. Scott sings of giving up or sacrificing the little incidentals of life, so as to be able to encounter true experience. It's then he sings, that it all comes shining through. Renunciation is compensated by gain. The song leads to a "road of thunder", and to a skeleton on a mount. Scott shelters his diction with an authoritative downness, as though the words are too heavy to fully lift into hearing. It's a compellingly stark vocal take, the tone again nursed by Mark Knopfler's plaintive guitar playing, and the lyric is lit up by Scott's searchingly redemptive inflections. Both songs should be considered as elegies which accommodate the depersonalised feelings common to individuals living in a despiritualized epoch.

These two songs are a little known expression of Scott's work, and were clearly experiments out of which *Tilt* was to evolve. That they differ in their musical texture from the material on *Tilt*, only goes to highlight their individual merit. Thematically, their closest analogue in Scott's work is "The Plague", a tormented daybreak lyric full of agonized remorse, which served as the B-side to his 1967 single, "Jackie". Other than this tenuously strained link, the two songs are foregrounded in Scott's mode of individually won spiritual existentialism. They give isolated voice to what is for him a continuous journey. They are additionally interesting as they are the lyrics with which Scott chose to break a decade's silence, in which he appears never to have been heard, seen by the media, or to have given a single interview. "Man From Reno" was Scott's resurrection, and so it provides access to his inner preoccupations, even if the song was written for a French-language film starring Isabelle Adjani. The reason for the single's not being released in England was explained by Scott's management as due to its not representing the sound of the still unreleased *Tilt*.

It's March, and today a stucco-coloured, luminously patchy sky sits above the city. So much goes on in London, and whoever we are, and whatever we do, we are a very small part of the molecular hologram. We occupy our little space in the whole. We are all of us words in a story that changes every day, and which in turn can never be completed. At this moment, a Wardour Street prostitute is leading a client into her room, somebody else is sitting dazed by an HIV diagnosis, somebody else is buying a CD, somebody is revising a novel, and someone is writing this book about Scott Walker. The possible diversities of life are inexhaustible. Our individual moment is all-inclusive to consciousness. We contribute our part, and qualitatively our work reflects our lives. There's disposable work, and work that outlives its individual creator. William Blake wrote that "Eternity is in love with the productions of Time", by which I think he meant that spiritual activity celebrates man's temporal achievements. I think he also intends to say that we should work while we have the opportunities presented by time.

This afternoon, Scott is somewhere, and I am somewhere else, joined to him by the quirkily empathetic tangent this book pursues. I reflect on how much of my thinking is occupied by a man who remains an enigma. Is this how the dead think about the living, and the living about the dead? And is our vehicle for doing so, the imagination?

Back to Scott's romanticism. Stage stars have in the course of the twentieth century become the apotheoses of contemporary culture. Television has both demystified and enhanced their iconic status, and Scott's extraordinarily fine looks quickly won him a following as a complementarity to his voice. The downward looking, shiveringly introverted, and painfully shy singer, his features framed by a heavy blond fringe, looked like the embodiment of the romantic ideal. At a time when poets had elected to look like accountants, an appearance they continue to maintain, Scott was a reminder of the sensitive man, feminized to a degree that hinted at the androgyne. Scott's inherently romantic sensibility has never been extinguished, and is the subtle particle X that lifts the material on *Tilt* out of a potentially nihilistic void.

One of Scott's perennially neglected songs, "The Plague", demands attention in terms of his recording history, in that its buried themes have resurfaced decades later in Scott's nineties work. Marc Almond's adoption of the song, and his recording of it on *A Woman's Story*, suggests that Almond tied Scott's metaphysical malaise to the endemic outbreak of AIDS in the early years of the eighties, at a time when the virus was being metaphorically likened to a plague. Scott's inspiration for his 1967 composition, may have come through reading Albert Camus' novel *The Plague*, as Scott is a professed Camus admirer, and the French writer's popularity had been assimilated to British culture in the course of the sixties.

"The Plague", with its introduction of tollingly ominous bells into its musical components, is one of Scott's most anguished compositions, and a song in which he ruthlessly exposes himself as the identifiable subject. "I've spent many a night lying on my back/Waiting for the dawn to pierce the crack/In the ceiling hanging from the sky", Scott sings, with the pained authenticity of somebody crisised into panic at the unspecifiable anxiety generated by being. The song is unpretentiously solemn, and Scott evokes the common psychological longing of a return to the innocence of childhood, as a way out of the spiritual staining that comes as a consequence of experience. It's a theme to which he gives voice in "Young Man

Cried", and "Boy Child", and one which is deeply impacted into the grain of "The Plague". Scott's frustrated longing is expressed as: "And I envied the boy who grabbed the toy and ran away and found a joy, while I stood in the shadows wondering why." As we grow older, we often insight youth as having represented a state where reflective pain is absent. By way of contrast, the experience that has brought Scott to writing "The Plague", is like a twisted knot of psychic terror. "The Plague" is another song that belongs to Scott's nocturnal repertoire, and one in which night hallucinations are prominent: "In the mirror of the night I see/A face that's staring down at me/Like a falling star burns itself out", he delivers with the urgent insistence of somebody possessed. The song is unremittingly earnest in its narration of inner crises, and may be seen as a formative example of the more universalized anxiety that Scott was much later to bring to *Tilt*.

"The Plague". The song was suitably underworlded as the flip-side to "Jackie", the controversial single with which Scott made chart-tracks in 1967. The number has always lived in ecliptical shadow, as the down-side or B-side of a 7" vinyl single. "The Plague" is like a black sun which has been buried for decades in Scott's obscurer archives. When I listen to it, I think of Wordsworth's lines in "Resolution And Independence": "We poets in our youth begin in gladness/And thereof come in the end despondency and madness."

Who is Scott now in relation to the individual who wrote "The Plague"? The two clips from his live TV performances in 1995 suggest that his introspection has deepened. The singer looked nervously fragile, and recently dropped in from a space in which one suspects the audience wouldn't feel comfortable. If plague represents for Scott, the notion of man's inner disquiet as pathology, then the artist is clearly still caught in the malaise's inexorable hold.

The idea of the socially dysfunctional artist, living at an edge to society, and embodying in every aspect the position of the outsider, may form a part of the romantic myth of suffering, but it is also an unenviable truth. Artistic populism is invariably the instrument that orchestrates attention, but outside of the popularity it generates, the voice of the imagination persists. Scott belongs to the infinitely richer expression of imagination, an art that takes longer to come through, but which proves in the end to be the durable medium.

"Man From Reno" had been Scott's first single for a decade, and the song appeared haloed by the isolation that the artist had suffered in the dead years. Politically, and socially, the eighties had represented tyrannical materialism, with Thatcher and Reagan attempting a chronically analgesic repression of individual freedom. Imagination had found itself under wraps, and any attempt at recovery has been a slow one. The eighties wasn't a decade likely to prove sympathetic to Scott's music, and in a way it's understandable that he disappeared into psychic exile to avoid its deadening economic dialectic. Given that Scott has almost no American market, response to his work is sited in Britain and Europe. The nineties have offered no shift away from materialism, but in consolidating anti-imaginative values, have at least allowed for some artistic reaction to a uniformly restrictive ethos, and the latter give has made an album like *Tilt* appear possible, as an antidote to a grey climate. Without intentionally placing *Tilt* in time, Scott has nonetheless devised a record that perfectly reflects its interior tensions. *Tilt* is no more about the nineties than J.G. Ballard's novel, *Cocaine Nights*, or John Ashbery's collection of poems, *Can You Hear Bird*, but its undercurrent translates direct into the age. Imagination interprets the future in a way that makes ideology redundant.

It's not that *Tilt*, or any of Scott's work, is outside mainstream interests, it's more that his creativity represents the inner heart of the ethos. It's a problem that a certain category of writer encounters, and that is one of transparent vision: the ability to transcend the age in which the work is delivered, while remaining central to it. I don't feel that a finer work than *Tilt* has evolved from the protean frontiers of pop, and I suspect too that *Tilt* will be translated into the musical currency of future generations, in the way that Lautréamont's *Maldoror* has come to appeal to successive generations of subversively indie youth.

Isidore Ducasse, the Comte de Lautréamont, and Noel Scott Engel, the singer Scott Walker. I began this book by bringing into play their likenesses, their penchant for pseudonyms, and their mutually shared love of the anonymous privacy surrounding the creative act. Both artists obtain to anorexic biographies, and neither will be subsumed by media reductionism. *Maldoror*, as a book, has threatened everyone who has come to its pages with loss of orientation, and with a violently juxtaposed image world, in which reality is perceived as something like "the meeting between a sewing-machine and an umbrella". Scott's *Tilt* also up-ends most conceptions of contemporary pop, and we may initially resist its voice instrumentation and off-centre lyrics. There's no easy way in, the listener wins a place in the music by bringing a receptivity to the work proportionate to its inspirational content. When that balance is achieved we begin to hear *Tilt*.

It's another Monday, and March is breaking into heady pink flower. It's a time of the year when London parks invite the memory of old loves, names we have let go to others, and they to still others in the remorseless chain of gain and loss, which signifies love. Somebody has lost an Angelica, or Genevieve, to use names from

Scott's songs, while someone else may be winning a Joanna, or Jackie, at this moment. Romance is one of the few inextinguishable dominants inherited by every age. Twenty years ago, and thirty years ago, teenage girls walked through London's parks fantasising about how it would be to find love in Scott's arms. Each day girls pulled searing arrows out of their hearts, and stared at the cut-outs on their walls, and at the album sleeves on which Scott is depicted. Their longing ached in the deep unrequited way that infatuation with an idol brings. There wasn't any way of consummating their romantic yearning for impossible love.

Where are those girls today at the moment in which I am writing *Another Tear Falls?* Are they the ones who went out and purchased *Tilt* on its release, and assisted Scott in regaining a place in the Albums charts? Will they always feel a tiny pocket of regret in their hearts that their love for Scott will be endlessly unrequited? Scott, who was the guardian of their youthful dreams, has matured into the enigmatic recluse whose voice keeps an elegiac watch on the passing years.

The propensity to cultivate solitude, as a compensation for rejection of the adult world, often forms part of a youthful death wish. What at first sight may have appeared as a blue-mooded affectation on Scott's part – the youthful romantic in love with death – never shifted, and Scott instead of being disinherited from his creative ideal, began the deepening process which has allowed his work to grow into the sombre proportions of *Tilt*. Artists in the pop world rarely expand their youthfully adopted sound into serious art expression. On the contrary, they often reach middle-age, and then attempt the inevitable reversion to their roots sound, with all the inauthenticity that such lack of development suggests. It would be like Scott deciding at the age of fifty to recreate an album comparable to the sound that the Walker Brothers achieved in 1966 with *Portrait*.

If Scott chooses to build on *Tilt*, then we can be certain that his new material will reflect the continuity of his inner journey. The poet, Rainer Maria Rilke, spoke of how "we are always becoming", in our spiritual destiny, and Scott's awareness of inner freedom has him attach his work to a similar mode of addressing intrinsic values.

I want to go back in time to some of Scott's lesser known songs, which are nonetheless integral to his development as an artist. The first of these is the John Stewart song, "After The Lights Go Out", an umbrageously lowlight song that was appropriately released as the B-side to the Walker Brothers' 1966 hit, "The Sun Ain't Gonna Shine Anymore".

"After The Lights Go Out" is a song perfectly suited to Scott's voice, but more than that it reads like a blueprint to some of the preoccupations that would concern him in coming to write and record his own material. The song takes as its nocturnal theme loneliness, and vignettes an abandoned lover reflecting on his solitary life, and the various irritants to his nerves occasioned by neighbours, as the nights starts to come on. Interestingly this composition highlights the voyeuristic and spectatorial aspects of Scott's psychology that were to play such a dominant role in his self-compositions. The permeable domestic boundaries which are so much a feature of Scott's early writings, are templated in this prototypical example of Scott's adopting a naturally melancholy persona. John Stewart's lyrics are pedestrian, but Scott manages to impart a meaningful destiny to the song. "After The Lights Go Out" is one of those four minutes of pop mastery to which Scott has given a durable legacy. "As the sun goes down/My silent little room is growing dim", he sings in that unforgettable baritone, before confirming the song's depressive theme: "And the man next door/Is saying what a lousy day it's been". The lyrics find little that is original to say, but Scott internalizes the grey-mood melodrama of a song devoted to a lover's dreading the advent of night. "I don't look for her/I find her in the shadow of my mind", Scott empathises, as though he knows the problem all too well. There's something about this melodic lament, with its blue-grained sense of rejection, that speaks for sixties pop, and perhaps it's the title of the song that centrestages associations with Scott. "After The Lights Go Out" is as a pop construct seminal to Scott's development as a songwriter. The song seems to have provided a flooring on which Scott was to build songs like "Montague Terrace In Blue". In John Stewart's song, an overheard audible detail of a girl downstairs crying for her lover, was later to resurface in Scott's "Montague Terrace In Blue", in the richer lyric texture of: "The girl across the hall makes love/Her thighs lie cold like shattered stone".

Let me extend the analogy. There are artists who stay with one vision all their lives. They connect with a predominant archetypal expression, and remain true to the dominant in a private mythology. The painter, Francis Bacon, typifies this mode of obsessive creativity. There's little contrast in Bacon's work in a time period spanning fifty years. He keeps with the image of anatomical distortion right through his career. There are modifications along the way, but these are small. You could argue the same for Ted Hughes' poetry. An early shamanic vision rooted in primal origins forms the insistently tenacious drum-roll of Hughes' work. Consciousness, and its dialogue with the elemental kingdom has fuelled the thrust of Hughes' poetry over four hugely prolific decades.

With Scott it is the same process. A youthful apprehension of emotionally universalized suffering, has remained the dynamic instructing his creativity. You could call it existential pessimism, or disillusioned romanticism. They are the same, for both are derived from spiritual origins, or the metaphysical malaise that had Baudelaire write *My Heart Laid Bare*. Scott's vision of life seems to have remained consistent. It is this, which in part, has contributed to his genius.

Interviewed in 1984, Scott was typically reserved about what his songs could mean to others, and offered no encouragement in the pursuit of admiring his songwriting capabilities. Pressed for an answer, he will say: "I'm a little loath to discuss material. It's so damn hard, you know, and it brings it all back to me... and I feel unlucky when I have to discuss it." The very fact of Scott's feeling unlucky about aspects of his career suggests as always a wound he is unwilling to discuss. But it also implies a certain reverence on the artist's part for his peculiar gift. If we value something deeply we may fear defusing its contents through critical analysis. We may also be afraid the gift will desert us if we show it disrespect. And so we may choose to keep inspiration secret. Writing clearly doesn't come easy to Scott, and so he may feel a need to shelter his creation.

It seems futile to hope that Scott would ever participate in this book. As I doubt there will ever be a comprehensive biography of Scott Walker in his lifetime, I'm consoled by the realisation that Jean Genet similarly resisted biographical autopsy. Nobody in Genet's lifetime ever established his true date of birth. He was always an unresolvable mystery to his readers and admirers. In Genet's comparatively few interviews, he like Scott rarely contributed personal confessions. He would enumerate on almost nothing relating to his past. It wasn't until after Genet's death, that Edmund White began work on his monumental biography of the French writer. But even given White's literary sass, and his brilliant evocation of his subject, we feel after reading seven hundred pages of *Genet*, that even in death the convict has covered his traces.

What I am in dialogue with are those inner aspects of Scott which seem to meet with their external correlatives. If you know nothing about Jean Genet, then reading *Our Lady Of The Flowers*, will provide an alarming insight into his psychology. The man will have given you access to almost everything meaningful in his life at the time of writing the book. Through imagination he will have excavated his interior. Genet's lyricism stands as a metaphor for his unconfessed life. I believe that the same applies to Scott, and that a sensitive reading of his work points to the man's more serious preoccupations. Although an artist is never totally the sum of his work, and although his way of relating to the world may differ radically from how he presents ideas in his chosen art, there will always remain an identifiably subjective centre to the creative product. There will be an irreducible sympathy co-existent between the artist and his work. One is spotlit by the other.

The rain's coming on today in articulate monotone. The cherry trees have put on pink dresses, and March is almost through. I imagine Scott is aware of cherry blossom in its extravagant, diffuse pinks, as the flowers tumble into London's parks and gardens. Jean Genet was once imprisoned for stealing roses from a cemetery. You would expect a poet to take the risk.

Scott's work has always studiously circumvented the idea of entertainment. Even when the Walker Brothers were at their most popular, Scott's voice, while it invited admiring attention, was never an entertainer's voice. There's a reserved, self-reflective quality to his intonation, and a seriousness too, that don't translate into commercial appeal. When we hear Scott singing, we're arrested by his vocal qualities, and in fact stopped in our tracks by the gravity of the singing voice. There's no way in which we can eliminate the voice from hearing. But the concerned, earnestly focused constituents of his tone are too much like the real thing for comfort. We listen to Scott when we want to discover truths about ourselves. Presumably Scott sings in order to clarify the arrangement of furniture in his psyche.

Who remembers forgotten pop songs? We could ask the same question about the wooden sea of out of print novels which have slipped into oblivion over the centuries. A minor self-composition like Scott's "Deadlier Than The Male", originally released as the soundtrack to a film of the same name, begs the question will anyone ever again, outside of a circle of devotees, listen to such material? Issued as a single in 1966, the song occupies all of 2.28, with the music written by Johnny Franz. It's the A-side to Scott's funereally beautiful "Archangel", and offers one of the most impressively compressed vocals delivered on a pop song. Scott's vocal insight is awesome in his deadly controlled delivery. He sings like an assassin who has only one shot with which to find his mark, and carries it through with exemplary panache. The song isn't the sort of composition the listener enters in order to sit down and claim it for his own. On the contrary, we surf the song's filmic direction, as though its contents should be absorbed without going too deep. In this instance, Scott's voice is too big for the fragile lyrics. He's telling us in the minimal time-frame, that "The smile that made a dream begin, clouds your vision/It's just the shadow of a dream that you're living in", but his seriousness is asking too much of minor lyrics. It's the disparity between voice and contents that breaks the song. Outwardly, the number has all the ingredients of a Scott Walker song, but inwardly it lacks gravity and conviction. But in listening to "Deadlier Than The Male", we ask the song to provide a sense of false redemption. Scott's voice sounds heroically up there in the thunder clouds, as he asserts: "I walk in streets you've never known, when the night comes/Sitting in places that you go, hoping she'll be there", and for the moment of engagement with the song, we suspend all possible alternatives to the story. There is only Scott's voice in that instant, and we take it on trust.

I suppose we ask of pop songs the impossible, and that is that they restore to us our youth. We go on listening to them in order to evoke associative memories, and because they trigger in us a sense of psychic retrieval. It's not that we're trying to reverse time in the process of listening, it's more that we're attempting to resituate ourselves in a place that we've never left. We feel protected by entering into the timeless present that song provides. In Jean-Paul Sartre's novel *Nausea*, a book pertinent to Scott's existentialism, the novel's protagonist, Antoine Roquentin, only loses his sense of debilitating alienation when he goes through the ritual of listening to a favourite record. When the singer provides the line, "One of these days you'll miss me honey", so Roquentin's angst disappears into temporary remission. It's a trick that we've all learnt for ourselves. We play a record, arguably one of Scott's, and our mood finds confirmation through the voice.

Scott's minor songs, like "The Gentle Rain", "Turn Out The Moon", "Deadlier Than The Male", or "Genevieve", are probably only played by real enthusiasts. As there is little likelihood of Scott ever returning to live performance, then we are faced with the realisation that he may never sing any of his songs again. In this respect, we can regard Scott's work as historic. All of it belongs to the singer's past. It is not a repertoire subject to live interpretation, and so nothing in his oeuvre will ever again enter into real time. Scott has situated his work in what I have chosen to call the timeless present, and that is the illusion created by the recorded voice that it has defied age, and is always immediate to our listening. Scott's reissues have a Dorian Gray quality to them, in that neither the original artwork nor the voice has ever changed. But unlike Wilde's Dorian Gray, I suspect Scott cares nothing for the perpetuation of this youthful illusion. When Johnny Franz first heard a tape of Scott singing "Love Her", thirty-three years ago in his Philips office, he was overwhelmed by a voice that occupied all his hearing. I can play "Love Her" today, and feel the same, only that now Scott has three decades of work behind him, and has travelled through time with the psychological and biological changes that the journey entails.

A Friday brings to an end the seventh chapter of our attempt to elucidate the enigmatic Scott. Will he always remain the elusive figure in an inconclusive fiction, and am I complicitous in helping to maintain the legend of the ultimate recluse? True to London weather, it's raining big flashy crystals today. March showers. I like the feel of the rain on the backs of my hands. The hits are stingingly cold. The rain attracts those who are looking for inspiration through its companioning solace. It often brings out the different, as well as snails. There's a good chance that Scott may be out in the opportune day rain. He's probably one of those who enters into a conspiratorial pact with the rain. Rain is like a halo to the depressed. It establishes a bright light without erasing a grey cloud ceiling. I imagine that's Scott's weather, for it's tonic to the essentially sad. I shall walk from one chapter to the next with wet footsteps.

WALKING IN THE RAIN

I've crossed over from one chapter to the next, in the rain. The title of this section is a throwback to what was to be the final Walker Brothers single, in 1967, a version of the Phil Spector classic originally covered by the Ronettes, and – appropriately for Scott – called "Walking In The Rain". For all its lack of chart success, and the critical indifference surrounding its release, it deserved better. Scott applies an epic delivery to the song, and the arrangement is awesomely complementary to the voice. The song may have lacked chart vitality at the time of its release, because it is too short, and doesn't permit Scott an extended overview of the mood-take. There's not enough of the song for Scott to gain vocal ascendancy, and after two choruses the number fades out to the atmospheric sound effect of stormy rain. Scott is denied purchase on what is a superior pop song, and a mood-theme ideally suited to his voice, however exemplary his treatment of what is in fact a miniature. We go on waiting for the song's continuity in the silence that succeeds it; the void which for a singer represents death. It's as though the singer has slipped off the edge of the world. His breathing space occupies 3.26.

"Walking In The Rain" happened for Scott in 1967. "In my end is my beginning", T.S. Eliot writes in "East Coker", and there's an authority to that line which speaks for all creativity. If the song, "Walking In The Rain", was effectively Scott's valediction to the pop ethos, then the exit it marked allowed him for the ensuing three years to explore a license of artistic freedom. The perennial problem for Scott is that time within the pop world is measured by commercial success, and that while he was permitted a degree of creative freedom between 1967–70, that privilege was immediately rescinded once his albums stopped selling. Success is expensive, and Scott on disbanding the Walker Brothers in 1967, was broke for reasons on which he was to expound: "The money went because I wanted the group to become as big as The Beatles or The Rolling Stones", he commented. "But it required us to act as big stars and big stars don't work every night in Britain. Apart from a trip to Japan we didn't work a lot abroad, and percentages from records were low... Then there were bills for suits that got torn every night we played, hotel bills, big drinks bills and entertainment bills. We came out with no money."

One doesn't associate Scott with materialism. There is the story of how at the height of his fame, and without even the money to buy food, he was to go into Philips' offices and to come out grateful for a loan of five pounds. Scott's creativity is an example of aesthetic asceticism. Artists need luxuries and not necessities, this is a proven paradigm. But they also need to live.

Rain has been a dominant mood in this book, or Scott's blue book. Rain has been the music to which it has been written. It's the morbid weather that seeps into all melancholic songs and poems. Baudelaire delighted in its spleen-inducing contents. The American poet, Weldon Kees, who disappeared off Golden Gate Bridge, reached his finest lyricism in his poem, "The Umbrella". Another disappearing act. Kees' car was found at the entrance to Golden Gate Bridge, but his body was never recovered. He goes on disappearing. The American poet, Hart Crane, took his body with him when he jumped from the stern of the Orizaba into the Caribbean Ocean. Scott may well prove to be an instinctual survivor, one of life's disappearing acts who stays.

Let's bring Scott back into contemporary focus. There's little recognition comes from making an album like *Tilt*. After the initial reviews, or the lack of them, an album generates sales by word of mouth, and through a fan-based dynamic. Feedback if it exists, is channelled by admirers who are friends, but the transmitted current isn't going to blow Scott away, or make a dark period lighter. In fact, it's unlikely to touch him at all. People don't usually make overt response to serious records or books. They take them inside themselves and keep them there as part of their interior. The after-glow isn't buzzy, or uplifting. Scott's life wouldn't have altered outwardly in any way as a consequence of releasing *Tilt*. It's his inner life which would have been touched by the release. Something which had been a part of Scott would have gone out into the world, and so his inner axis would have changed. Ezra Pound likened the process of publishing a book of poetry to dropping a rose petal into the Grand Canyon and listening for the echo. The same goes for serious music. The positive side to this, is that what is truly good, does eventually arrive, no matter its hazardous journey underground before finding acclaim. I suppose Scott got it right on "Patriot", with the lines, "The good news you cannot refuse/The bad news is there is no news". What is popular in its time is often as quickly dispensable, as it is disposable. True work often anticipates a future in which the artist is unable to participate. Scott has received some critical recognition for *Tilt*, although most reviewers felt uncomfortable with its unflinchingly bare-nerved dynamic. When an artist's work is rejected, its creator may radically lose self-confidence, and draw a defensive screen between himself and the work by dissociating from his creation. This event usually takes place in silence and dejection. Jean Genet once claimed that he hadn't smiled for twenty years. He had seen through the illusion of his work. He had seen that there was nobody on the other side of the page on which he had written. His books couldn't help him, and so he deserted them; he became somebody else, and convinced himself of the lie.

Has Scott participated in a similar process of disidentification? Does he remember himself sometimes, and return to his creative identity? When he reclaims his voice, it must be like the return of the lost, and the instrument is unlikely to prove immediately rehabitable. There would be a reluctance at first on both parts, the artist's and the instrument's. Scott would be frightened that his voice would let him down, or that it had assumed a different vocal fingerprint. These are big issues, and they can generate enough fear to stop anyone going back into the studio. Writers sometimes get psychologically blocked. It can happen to singers too. Scott and his voice have undergone a strained, uneasy marriage.

A book, like a record, is a work isolated in time. If like most singles released today, I could remix the writing five or six times, I would have the chance to present the contents in a multi-aspected form. There would be five takes of my particular book. Five different ways in which to locate Scott.

Scott has broken interview silence on very few occasions in the past twenty years. His policy of refusing to comment on his personal life reminds me of a similar strategy adopted by the American expatriate writer, Paul Bowles. From his Tangier base, Bowles has resolutely refused to comment on his ambiguous sexual orientation, or his estranged relations to his wife Jane, whose work continues to enjoy a posthumous cult following. Scott's interviews for *Tilt* were conducted in his manager's offices at Holland Park. There is no stepping into Scott's private space.

From 1964–1998. What is it that keeps Scott's fans loyal? It would be easy to say the voice, and to qualify the attraction in terms of the fineness of the instrument. But there's a deeper mystery attached to the life of an enduring icon, and it has got to do with how we relate to archetypes. Pop icons are like transgenic implants into the psyche. We relate to the ideals they collectivize, and empathise with aspects of their archetypal significance. Scott symbolises the youth who disappears, and the mystery of the undying one. We all part with our youth reluctantly, and go on retrieving youthful memories as a source of bittersweet consolation. In the same way, we go on listening to Scott's voice as an identification with this process. We may call on it in times of crisis, and summon it to our individual needs. Playing a record is like a magical invocation. We conjure voice into our presence.

The drug references in Scott's lyrics, which were so liberally distributed throughout the material on *Climate Of Hunter*, are also there on *Tilt*. Scott's later songs seem to codify a secret junky language. On "Rosary", we encounter references like, "With all of the trembling vein/that you can bare", and "Put it in lines across the room/But we'll never stop it pimpling", which seem to imply cryptic hints of drugs representing an alternative reality. We're unlikely to learn of Scott's relations to drugs, and they may be no more than that of a fictional identity with the outsider.

Here I am on a London Tuesday anticipating April. The sky's the colour of a funeral monument. If the clouds weren't moving, they could be headstones scattered across Highgate cemetery. No rain, and the flower-stall boasts canary-yellow tulips, as well as scarlet and purple. There's a sense of ecological shift. It's warm, although the sky gives nothing away of the big blue spaces on the other side of the clouds.

Scott's masterpiece, *Tilt*, is being played by somebody in London at this moment. It's a comforting thought that someone is taking refuge in discomfort. That person is tailoring the music to their lowlight mood. Scott's part in the process stopped in the recording studio, but he may be alive in Paris, St. John's Wood, or Amsterdam, as I write. His disembodied voice may be on repeat.

Back in 1984, Scott will say: "The '70s were a dry gulch, but now everyone can make the record they want, if they want to make it." And he will go on to reflect in the same interview: "You've not had people like Costello or Almond making records before – that's what makes this time different. In the '70s there were good records and maybe there were moments like the Sex Pistols. But now, if they can pull it off, they can do it. Before there was an inability to pull it off. That was my problem."

Jump a decade, and Scott seems with *Tilt* to have made the sort of individually uncompromising record to which he has always aspired. What punk, as a music genre succeeded in doing, was to blow apart the formulaic parameters which had previously defined pop. If the offensive auto-destructed, then punk at least erased the notion of pop music being considered primarily an entertainer's vehicle. Scott, whose career had been restrained in the sixties, and seventies, by the need to compromise over material that was considered uncommercial, was of course to benefit indirectly from punk. Ironically, the liberated decades which have followed on from punk have seen Scott at his least prolific. It's almost as though his perverse response to indie liberation has been to freeze into contracted silence.

Is Scott Walker best seen as a study in the psychopathology of creativity, or is he simply an eccentric perfectionist, an artist who waits his time without feeling any real urgency to communicate to an audience? What seems to suggest that the latter theory is untrue is the intensity and anxiety that Scott brings to each new project. It's not that the man or his work relocates from a passive space. Scott doesn't appear or sound like a man whose periods of inactivity have involved relaxation or attempts at self-harmony. On the contrary he seems like someone who has to engage in a lot of self-repair in order to assume the concentrated focus necessary to initiate the writing and recording of new material. Does each of Scott's later albums represent the singer's return from a dysfunctionally depressive state to a short-lived period of creative activity? Is Scott at this moment incapable of working, or is he simply not interested in the proposition?

Any book that attempts to approach Scott on a deep level, will by the nature of its subject be correspondingly weird. You simply can't put Scott's outsidership into chronology. The facts of a life may have a chronological basis, but inner dictates don't belong to time. Scott's life as we know it, is no more rich in external events than anyone else's, excepting the brief period in the sixties when he found himself the subject of teenage adulation. And even then, Scott's existence was never the paradigm of excessive libertine behaviour, associated with pop stars of the period. He had at the time found himself involved in the beginnings of a music scene that had never before demanded such media attention. It wasn't Scott's world, but his heavy drinking would probably have existed independent of his being caught up in a pressurized industry. Scott's sensitivity and natural state of anxiety translate themselves into dependency.

The Scott who consumed a bottle of vodka in the studio, while cutting his vocal take of "I Still See You", has probably always manifested dependent behaviour. Alcohol or drugs are a means of stepping off the reality bridge without drowning in the manner of Hart Crane or Weldon Kees. Swimming in a sea of alcohol means going against the current. It is a process of slowing the self in heavy water. Alcohol deadens time. It kills momentum. You can be in clear vision one moment, and blackout the next. Scott has at times killed creative possibilities through alcohol. Malcolm Lowry wrote *Under*

The Volcano, while hallucinating on mescal. The French singer Serge Gainsbourg was never sober. There is a history of alcohol- and drug-induced creativity, which numbers Scott Walker in its exhaustive inventory of the semi-drowned. Scott has already dissolved big chunks of time. Time is eroded by alcohol in the way of soluble aspirin in water. Great registers of being disappear in the process. Scott, who can't retrieve lost time, has instead converted the loss into the bewilderingly estranged landscape that comprises *Tilt*. Only someone emerging into the sort of survivor landscape depicted by J.G. Ballard in novels like *The Atrocity Exhibition* and *Crash*, could have recorded the sort of post-human assemblage that *Tilt* represents as a signpost to cultural apocalypse. It's as though Scott has touched on the fault-line leading to earthquake. The deconstructive chaos that has run co-existent with the twentieth century has increased in momentum, and we have grown in part to be the disinherited, urbanly damaged creatures who inhabit an exhausted planet. *Tilt* can be heard as a lament for the despiritualized. The album concerns itself with the oppositional energies between personal values, and the depersonalized ethos instated by political totalitarianism. Man's innocence and man's freedom have been systematically reduced by manipulative ideologies. Scott's portrayal of modes of physical torture on *Tilt* is of course even more dangerously mirrored by loss of spiritual freedom. That the final line of the album should be "I gotta quit", isn't just a personal exit from the work, it's a suggestion on Scott's part that we're all on the way out. T.S. Eliot's inconclusively chaotic ending to *The Waste Land*, "London Bridge is falling down..." carries the same portentous stamp of cultural breakdown. In terms of imaginative apprehension London Bridge was collapsing as Eliot brought his poem to an unresolved end. Any vision that searches for unity will see the same debris happening all over again in a cultural free-fall of imagery. *Tilt* is inextricably linked to this visionary process. It touches on nerve-codes that transmit a light into the abyss.

I've just come back from the big Francis Bacon retrospective at the Hayward Gallery. It's an exhibition that concentrates on Bacon's obsession with the body, or distorted anatomy. Bacon often seems to want to resituate internal organs as external phenomena. His subjects appear to undergo weird reversals of contents. They are all in a state of metamorphic distortion. Bacon allows for no contained bodies. His body paintings resemble savage autopsies. There's the feeling that Bacon fled from his paintings, like somebody escaping from a torched building. His refuge was alcohol. Bacon's viewers are correspondingly in flight from their voluntary confrontation with meat. They stay for so long, and then retreat into another space. Junkies, convulsive anatomies, flayed interiors, and self-portraits

---

framed against black are the images relayed by a Bacon exhibition. We're compelled to encounter these biopsical exhibits, and then go back to face an asymmetrically towered and gapped London skyline slung above a fast-moving, khaki-coloured river. The Thames today is the colour of army fatigues. Its undertow gulps at history, and swallows every sort of ephemera. The river is logoed with urban disjecta. Reflect on it, and your thoughts unravel into a sliding, historic collective. Everything, including bodies has been dumped at some stage into the muscled water pumping under Waterloo Bridge. This stained area of water forms an appropriate out-there mirror to Bacon's imploded autopsies.

It's not without a distinct feeling for shared metaphors, that Scott has likened some of the in-the-face music on *Tilt* as being comparable to Bacon's paintings. Both artists confront their public with the unconfrontable. Politics represents a continuous attempt to disguise injustices and atrocities committed on the apolitical. Politicians attempt to hide the bodies that the river and art bring to the surface. Because the imagination finds metaphors for the political arena, it is the true record of civilisation. *Tilt* evokes profound human suffering, and redeems it through artistic expression. It offers voice to the afflicted, and stands as an elegy for the anonymously persecuted. And it does that through unintentional means, and through comprising the often random associations that Scott has compounded into a funereal mosaic.

At the beginning of the twenties, it took a foreigner to London, T.S. Eliot, to evoke the city's multi-faceted spirit, in the way that the capital hadn't come alive in poetry since William Blake's prophetic work, Jerusalem. Eliot did this by a means of poetic cut-ups, and what today in music would be called sampling. He transposed the legitimate past into the unsanctioned present. In his own way, and in a musical context, Scott has made *Tilt* into the pop equivalent of *The Waste Land*.

What's the point in writing books if you don't entertain risk? The tenuous connections between *Tilt* and *The Waste Land* may appear overstated, but they bite on the same face of the apple. It's easy to miss contemporary happenings, particularly as they usually occur outside popular standards of media convention. They are usually permitted to surface only after their cutting edge has been polished smoother by the passing of time. To begin with the river obscures the real thing, and it is often indetectable from the litter of expended cans. Much later, the current brings it to shore, and its untarnished value begins to shine.

Scott had considered performing *Tilt* live at the Queen Elizabeth Hall in 1995, and the venue would have been appropriate, given its fronting on the river. Eliot wrote in *The Waste Land* of, "This music crept by me upon the waters." *Tilt* would have been the appropriate suite of music given ear to by the Thames, if the singer had acted on his latent desire to perform.

How Scott's reputation is read by posterity is probably irrelevant to the artist's concerns. Writers, singers and artists lose reputation, sometimes temporarily and sometimes for good. They may shift in or out of focus, or completely disappear. Critical climates change, and so do modes of popular expression. But if a work will live, it must anticipate a future independent of its creator. It will establish its own autonomy, and be around without vested back-up or self-protection. We can pretty well say that Scott has let all his solo work live without his support, and so there is a very good chance that it will continue to do so after his death. We have got used to the idea of Scott's music existing in his absence. He has in fact perfected the art of living posthumously. It is the voice which provides identity to Scott's oeuvre, while the man has effaced every recognisable feature of a public image.

Scott is a rare instance of a living artist maintaining a profile without any form of publicity. In the years subsequent to the release of *Tilt* (1995), the only brief mention of Scott has been in relation to his recording a Bob Dylan song, "I Threw It All Away", as part of the soundtrack to the movie *To Have And To Hold.* Reviewers were to single out his contribution as a film noir rendition of an undistinguished ballad, and to praise its gravity as another example of Scott's vocal artistry. But the man has dematerialized again, offering no clues as to his present identity.

If Scott has become the shy, anonymous stranger, whom nobody recognises in the crowd, then perhaps he has fulfilled his spiritual conviction that in order to realise our inner selves, we need to embody private, and not public identities. It was Julian Cope who attached the metaphor of "god-like genius" to Scott Walker, and in an archetypal sense all creativity relates to a presiding deity. If there is a psychic guardian in the crowd for Scott, then it's probably Orpheus. An ideal record sleeve for one of his early solo albums would have been a detail from *Lamentation Of Orpheus* (1896), by Alexandre Séon, a painting which hangs in the Musée d'Orsay in Paris. In the painting, a long-haired, androgynous Orpheus lies with one arm thrown over his eyes, and with his other arm he cradles a lyre against his torso. He represents the image of romantic youth shattered by individual destiny.

The Scott who used to drive a jeep across London, the youthful singer who would only fly if he was accompanied by a doctor, the defiant rebel who identified with Jean Genet, the suicidal

Scott, the beaten up and found Scott, the Scott who entered a monastery, the cabaret singer who requested absolute silence from his audience, these are some of the better known incidents of Scott's life. But even in their totality, they amount to little in terms of a life, and are only pointers to deeper psychological issues. Central to Scott's sensibility is non-compromise, and the rebel in him persists, no matter the consequences. Thirty years ago, Scott professed that Elvis Presley had the right voice to cover most of the Walker Brothers' big hits, and admitted a secret longing to produce the King. Scott stated this ambition over and above the possibly disastrous consequences that such a liaison could have had on his own career as a singer. "I couldn't care less if I didn't get to sing another note," Scott provided by way of defiance. Scott's complete absence of conforming to commercial guidelines has been an act of continuous rebellion.

The Scott who once wore the key from Quarr Monastery around his neck, has symbolically used that key to lock himself into silence. In his published letters, the Marquis de Sade relates how when he was imprisoned in the Bastille, he would hear his jailer unlocking a whole sequence of successive metal doors, before arriving with food at his cell. The assemblage of multiple locks was a device as much intended to impress on the Marquis his being unfit to mix with his fellow humans, as it was a contrivance of oppressive torture aimed at telling the prisoner that escape would prove impossible. Scott has voluntarily, as we know it, locked himself away from the world, and deepened his sense of seclusion from the public. His process has been the reverse of Sade's, in that not only has Scott enjoyed freedom as opposed to confinement, but he has lacked Sade's impulsive dynamic to use solitude as a trigger to prolific creativity. Sade filled his vacuum with words, as though he feared the imminent advent of insanity if he should stop writing. Sade's massive, intractable, and unreadably obscene novels were constructed by their author as a defence system against madness. Scott seems to have endured silence and solitude without feeling a compulsive need to create. If his behaviour sometimes seems removed from the human norm, then his anti-social traits are never savage in the manner of a Sade or Artaud. And something of a pronounced black humour permeates the interviews he gave in defence of *Tilt*, a humour that permits the singer to acknowledge the absurd in the face of total despair. Scott even appeared to welcome the notion of adverse criticism, seeing in the extreme reaction to his work a response preferable to that of critical indifference.

It's a Wednesday afternoon, and the sky's the colour of a black grape. The rain when it comes has the brilliant sparkle of April showers. Despite the fact that the rain arrives out of London's toxic air pollution, it still imparts a tonic and uplifting glow to the senses. Rain is best heard beneath a skylight, for then you get the whole zingy, rushed sound effects. Rain on a skylight sounds like a saucepan coming to the boil. It's best experienced while you're reading a poem by Frank O' Hara, or listening to Scott's deep melancholic strains. As the rain begins out of a cloud mass shaped like Africa, I'm reminded of John Keats' epitaph: "Here lies one whose name was writ in water." If Scott's in London, he will be experiencing the same rain, and even if it no longer inspires him to write songs direct from the experience, it will enter his sensory ambience.

And what of Coil as the late century purveyors of urban apocalypse? One could imagine Scott listening to their obliquely masterful evocations of a music that locates spirit within the industrial ethos. John Balance, and Peter Christopherson, the lyric and musical dynamic behind Coil are contenders for the river god's crown, as the Thames picks up on the evasive music that enticed Eliot's ear. Coil's non-ambient, but neurologically explorative music resembles a hologram of cultural references that connects somewhere with Scott's deepest inner concerns.

Tilt comprises Scott's supreme creative monument to date. This suite of songs represents his funeral music. In "Manhattan", he evokes, "Scalper in the lampglow/scalper on a chair/stick wiped shirt/and his arm somewhere", as though he is composing a body every bit as deformed as one of Bacon's anamorphs. Scott's political prisoners, who are tortured out of shape, in the context of his songs, have to redefine themselves through spirit. Scott's shredded, Olsonian poetics work like a scalpel on excess. He will give you nothing more than the inextinguishable light at man's interior. The one light that refuses to go out, because it cannot. Scott's sombreness is connected with transcendence.

There are passages in Scott's infrequent interviews, which put associations together, with the same sense of incongruity that he brings to his image juxtapositions in lyrics. In his 1984 interview, Scott will say: "Sometimes you think, maybe nobody's seen it this way before, and then... Maybe a good Lionel Ritchie or Michael Jackson record is as important. If they work – a record by John Coltrane or Michael Jackson can become the same thing. The finality of everything, if it's resonating in the same way, it's the same thing..."

Scott's manner of connecting the integrants of a song resembles his thought processes. He hits in at the centre from a series of seemingly accidental raids on consciousness. He arrives by tangential means at his discoveries.

Another Tear Falls

Is Scott the singer who threw it all away, or simply the solitary creator who has chosen to go it alone, and shed his entertainer's image like a snake its skin? Towards the end of his life Derek Jarman spoke of the problems he had encountered in endeavouring to make films expressive of ideas, rather than movies aimed at generating entertainment. Scott's problems run parallel to Derek Jarman's, in that both artists begin by disowning the premises on which entertainers build. Neither will forfeit integrity for commercial gain. Jarman's defiantly beautiful, subversively underground films in which the gay ideal is apotheosised, are constructed in ways that cross over to Scott's *Tilt*. Both are the works of singularly courageous individuals who have tapped into the disquieting current that runs through the twentieth century's furred arteries.

Entertainment as a medium rarely produces durable art. It's the stuff that glitters on the river's spine before being dragged under. When artists go in search of popularity, it usually means that they are willing to adjust their creative modalities to fit the boundaries of entertainment. The problem with the latter expression is that it is dependent on the artist's person to keep it alive. Good art lives independent of its creator. It's on this reef that so much pop music quickly founders.

Scott's biographers have rightly pointed out that today, little remains of the singer's sixties London. His drinking clubs like The Scotch of St James and the Cromwellian have disappeared, so too the Lotus House restaurant, and his old residence, Dudley Court. Geography changes like the cells in our bodies. Cities are assembled, disassembled and reassembled with cyclic regularity. A neighbourhood gets buried beneath a new superimposed facade, and money is the index which regulates the change. Scott's own collapsing inner defences are mirrored in the outer landscape. It's unlikely that Scott will ever again find an external nucleus in the city, in terms of being connected to a milieu, or a loosely described pop ethos. How he encounters the city now is as an outsider. He is free to be everybody and nobody, and to join the dispossessed through whom he speaks on *Tilt*. Scott, like so many sixties musicians achieved too much too soon, and experienced an immediate fame disproportionate to the work created. Success happened fast and often transiently to a generation unprepared for the consequences. It's psychologically hard to adjust to the transformation from private to public figure, and then to undergo the reverse process on the backwash of declining popularity. It's almost as though this should never have happened to Scott, for unlike so many jettisoned pop icons Scott was in possession of a voice and an inward-searching sensibility that seemed radically set apart from his contemporaries.

His despondent sense of not belonging to the music industry, and yet feeling compelled to periodically resituate himself in it is deep at the roots of his existential anxiety. It's as though having once tasted success, the aftertaste of its redolent illusion returns at intervals, and sends him back into the studio fighting with the awareness that it's another time, another place.

It's April, and the hawthorn trees are in abundant, musty, red flower. They've come alive in the London parks, and they smell of vanilla and semen. You can read a book in two days that took six years to write, or listen to a piece of music in an hour that took six months to complete in a studio. The reader or the listener is always at this advantage.

My book has grown out of years of earnest reflection on Scott's deepening solitude, and a lifelong appreciation of his voice. It has taken form in the early spring. I began this book on a day of persistent rain, and the rain is still crowding at the window, as I write. In our digital, information-highwayed cities we tend to forget the elements, and how deeply connected they are to the creative impulse. Listening to the rain may be the way in to a poem, a book, or a song. It brings thought to the surface of the skin, like goose-pimples bumped up by the cold.

No news from Scott, and so he continues to live as the enigmatic subject of fictional biography. I've been to the river today, and it's a troubled distillation of buried greens and greys. A ferry thugs downriver and its tourist passengers take in the uncompanionably concrete-faced skyline. We're all present in the now of that moment. The South Bank looks like a high-definition video still. "I don't believe reality exists," Derek Jarman said, in a late interview. None of us does. We're inner and outer creatures, and we exchange dimensions constantly.

Scott's work has survived the difficult decades, but where does that leave the artist? Work that's done isn't doing anything now for him, except generating small royalties. It must seem to him, like it all happened a lifetime ago to a taciturn, romantic young singer who became the acclaimed voice of the sixties. At times, Scott wakes up from the big sleep and attempts to reassemble the pieces into some form of continuity. We don't see him, and we don't know why this happens, but with instinctual genius, he has with *Tilt* created the ultimate pop record. It's a weird, off-kilter, apocalyptic suite of songs that situates us in the almost post-human future in which we are living. It's a work that could only have been written by an outsider.

A time to end this book on a rain-striped April day, with the river carrying a film of the sky on its back. If I waited on Waterloo Bridge long enough, would Scott eventually come by? Would he be amongst the crowds filing towards the South Bank complex, his dark shades protecting him from direct light? It's a crazy notion, the idea of waiting on Waterloo Bridge for Scott to materialise, but writing provokes those sort of unorthodox encounters. It ain't gonna stop raining. The river's indifferent to everything as it drags history forward. Scott's somewhere in this city, and probably not doing very much at all.

APPENDIX: TWO ORIGINAL ESSAYS

HEROIC GESTURES

Scott Walker, Frank Sinatra, Marc Almond

Somewhere in the history of torch singers, jazz singers, pop singers and crooners, if distinctions can be made in these always interchangeable categories of style, came a voice so inimitable in its heroic characteristics, that it was immediately recognized as an ideal for singers.

The voice was of course Scott Walker's, his rich baritone thrust applying itself to tearjerker pop ballads that were made to sound like arias colouring a compressed wall of orchestral sound. Songs like "Love Her", "Make It Easy On Yourself", "My Ship Is Coming In" and "The Sun Ain't Gonna Shine Anymore", were singles that arrested a sixties generation of blue-hearted lovers, looking for the consolation afforded by moody songs. And it isn't that Scott was without predecessors. Elvis Presley, Roy Orbison and Gene Pitney, to name only three, had all endeavoured to infuse the ballad with sovereign meaning, and to stagger the song's trajectory towards a vertical climactic axis.

But Gene Pitney's yearning for heroics, evidenced in songs like "Twenty Four Hours From Tulsa", falls considerably short of the vocal expertise that Walker brings to a comparable ballad like "Another Tear Falls". If the comparison appears considerably to Pitney's disadvantage, then it's at the expense of Walker's genius. Scott's beginnings, like his brooding literary concerns, and his aspirations to transcend the narrower parameters of pop music, are of course mirrored in Marc Almond's initial success with the electro-pop duet Soft Cell. Both were singers constrained by a medium not only dependent on youth culture, but also on the accessible hook of their material. And both had to earn commercial credibility before being allowed to experiment with their distinctive art forms within the study of singing.

In recollecting the initial premises of his friendship with Scott Walker during the 1960s, Jonathan King has pointed to Scott's intellectual passions at the time. "One of his fascinations," King tells us, "was Jean Genet and it was through discussing the character of this rather bizarre man that we found we had a lot in common."

Genet, who is empathetically incorporated into the homo-erotic dynamic of Marc Almond's creativity, finds his embodiment in Walker's psyche through shared aspects of inverted sainthood. Walker has consistently bypassed stardom in favour of pursuing artistic truth, in the way that Genet turned his back on the literary ethos of Paris and chose to situate his poetry in the underworld. Scott has progressively taken his work away from a commercial public, and in the process has demythicized his pop status, choosing instead to pursue an anonymous and largely reclusive life. Almond has in some ways followed suit, although his periodic invasion of the pop charts has served to give him an altogether more public profile. An integral artist, he has in order to secure recording contracts found it necessary to revitalize his pop instincts from time to time in order to finance the more serious aspects of his work.

At the height of the Walker Brothers' success in 1965, Scott found himself predominantly listening to jazz singers, and to the vocal stylists Frank Sinatra, Jack Jones and Tony Bennett. If the latter three are seen as great jazz-orientated pop singers, then it's more for their tonal colouring than their dramatic intentions. Sinatra has described his own style as *bel canto* (beautiful singing) without making a point of it. It's a genre of singing that initially fascinated Scott, and his recording of the classic "When Joanna Loved Me" on *Scott*, his first solo album, was succeeded by his mastery as an interpretative artist on *Scott Sings Songs From His TV Series*, and the later *The Moviegoer* album. If Sinatra moved beyond jazz singing by completely democratizing beats, and elongating rather than chopping phrases, so Walker applied a heroic romanticism to Sinatra's innovative technique. Sinatra has said of his own method: "You've got to get up and sing but still have enough down here to make your phrases much more understandable and elongated so that the entire thought of the song is there."

Walker's attempts to push baritone romanticism to overreach resulted in occasional vibrato, and for these reasons he was despatched to the voice coach Freddie Winrose in Denmark Street. Both Walker and Almond manifest sporadic tremor in their respective singing voices, and both push a song to its limits, and therefore risk failure. When the latter occurs, the resultant pitch is grandiose and promethean, whether it's Walker chasing the speculative notes of

"Impossible Dream" or Almond pursuing the operatic undertones of "She Took My Soul In Istanbul". If this tradition of singing has always existed in France, and Charles Aznavour and Jacques Brel were both formative influences on the two singers under consideration here, then it remains an outsider's art within the study of British and American pop.

In his introduction to the Scott Walker compilation *Boy Child (The Best Of 1967–70)*, Marc Almond credits his predecessor with having the supreme voice for the interpretation of the lonely song. "His voice," Almond writes, "has become a simile for all crooning deep tones and liquid vibrato," qualities he suggests that make it an ideal instrument to engage with the themes of death and desire. Almond who has recorded two of Walker's self-compositions "Big Louise" and "The Plague," has also covered many of the Brel songs that Walker originally made available in English on his first three solo albums. In no way emulative of Walker's singular genius as a singer, or the contracted, introverted sensibility behind the voice, Almond is in many ways Walker's only successor. Central to their achievements is an incontrovertible belief in the poetic lyric as sanctioning voice. Their repertoire is narrower than Sinatra's, and more reliant on applying a histrionic intensity to obsessive narratives of loss and death. What Almond shares with Sinatra is his casting of himself as the romantic lead of most of the love songs he sings, a role that Walker with his innate reticence is more reluctant to assume. Almond subjectively agonizes, whereas Walker sounds more comfortable behind the screen of third person heroics.

If Sinatra's egotism was what allowed him to portray himself in the roles of a desirous or defeated lover through his unfailing good taste in song, then it was his absolute seriousness as an artist that elevated him above his predecessors and contemporaries. It would be impossible ever again for a singer intending to make a durable art form out of the pop song, not to insight Sinatra as the prototype of believable expression. Sinatra confides, and we are his ear. His taste for standards has virtually defined the tenor of adult popular music. I have used the example of Sinatra as a measure from which both Walker and Almond depart, and they do so by a dramatic torchiness of phrasing, that while it is sometimes flawed, is nevertheless a sublime attempt to project poetic emotion into song. And this of course has something partly to do with singing out of gender, a shift of axis that applies more to Almond than to Walker, but is present in the work of both artists. Sinatra with his hats, and his complacency about being very much a man, an image unfalteringly sustained by his life, is true to the archetype of the male singer. Like his influences, Bing Crosby, Louis Armstrong and Mel Tormé, Sinatra was beyond suspicion, and it's his absolute certainty in terms of gender role that contributes to the voice sitting so comfortably with the masculine ideal.

Walker's outstanding good looks, all high cheekbones and aesthetic sensitivity were highlighted by the androgynous image made popular by the sixties. If his sexuality seemed ambiguous, then there were constant rumours of Scott being a nocturnal outlaw in search of the forbidden. Whatever Walker's sexual confusion, it's his state of deep inner disquiet that is communicated through singing. What he brought to his huge sixties ballads, and which is absent from the work of Sinatra and his imitators is a sense of using the contents of a song as a stage for unresolved anxiety. Sinatra comes to a song with the expectation of communicating to a norm through elevated speech. In getting himself right in the early hours Frank doesn't doubt that he's got the listener's acceptance. The love songs written for him are largely about the understandable ups ad downs in human relations. The lyrics eliminate the perversities, torments and inner crises that first Walker and then Almond were to implant into singing styles that seek redress from the angels. Sinatra's court of appeal is a bar, whereas Walker and Almond both address an etherealized dimension as much as they do a human plane of conflict.

It would be easy to say that Walker expresses the new ideal, and Sinatra the old, but Sinatra's method is the one still adopted by crooners, while Almond who struggles to maintain the heroic dimension in an age of horizontal singers remains the solitary proponent of Walker's style. Almond's failure to either confirm or deny public his putative gay sexuality has allowed him to take greater liberties in his choice of material, whether self-composed or chosen from the modern repertoire. He has for instance made a genuine feeling song of Aznavour's "What Makes A Man A Man", a number that Walker could have approached, but has clearly avoided for reasons of discretion. Almond has had no reservations about singing from a woman's point of view, and the impassioned dynamic he injects into a song like "A Woman's Story", sounds wholly authentic at the expense of women singers like Nina Simone who change the lyrics of a song to meet with gender conformity. Her disastrous attempt to switch the lyrics of the standard "When I Was A Young Man" to "When I Was A Young Girl" contrasts poorly with Almond's fluidity in adopting the feminine part in a song like "The Heel".

Walker approaches the issue with considerable more caution, preferring to narrate the story of the transsexual "Big Louise" in the third person. The songs's opening line "She stands all alone", situates the singer in his own isolated state. "Big Louise", the story of a man who has become a woman is the first pop song about a transsexual, and was arguably the blueprint to inspire Almond's concerns with gender mutation in the subject matter of his lyrics. Walker and Almond differ from the Sinatra generation of singers in that the controversial nature of their material places it outside the limitations of easy listening. And here the question arises as to the nature of compromise in singing. Has Sinatra been fulfilled by the relatively narrow lyric margins of his creative expression? Have the songbooks of Cole Porter, Rodgers and Hart, Irving Berlin and George and Ira Gershwin, to name but a few of the inspired songwriters at his disposal really touched on the darker issues at work in his psyche? While singing has been integral to Sinatra's life, I wonder whether there exists in the man a huge sense of frustration at the popularized material to which he has given that life.

Walker and Almond are romantics by reason of declaring their lives through their work. Unlike Sinatra, they have chosen to use the song as a medium of self-confession, an art facilitated by their abilities to write some of their own material. In Almond particularly, the "I" that we have called the romantic lead of the song is naked in its vulnerability. It's a very different lead from the structured persona given Sinatra by a songwriting team. Walker's self-regarding "Always Coming Back To You" or Almond's "I Who Never" are examples of self-composition that risk overexposing the artist, but remain great by the temerity of the dare. Romanticism whether it is in literature, art or music invariably invites a savage form of critical hostility from its detractors, who see the aggrandisement of the self as an unsuitable subject for artistic expression. The opposition between Dionysian and Apollonian approaches to creativity, that is the poles of inspiration and reason are brought into play here as the tension between subjective and objective styles of singing. Walker and Almond represent an imaginative affirmation of the individual as self-creator: the ongoing life is the source of the work. Sinatra and his imitators express a universal state of being, one which while it pertains to the self, is neither self-consciously personal, nor in any way dangerously confessional. A Sinatra record is likely to be assessed by the quality of the voice in relation to the suitability or unsuitability of the tunes recorded. An album by Walker or Almond permits the critic the additional arm of attacking the subject's personal life as it is reflected in the lyrics. And because of this both artists suffer for their work, and experience a sense of self-defeat when it is unduly disparaged. Critics scent blood whenever they set to on romantic vulnerability.

Walker's arrival at heroic voice was of course linked to his love of Phil Spector's insurgent wall of sound, an effect he set out to recreate with the assistance of producers like Ivor Raymonde, Reg Guest and Wally Stott. The voice was situated in front of a compressed Wagnerian crescendo, all of it contained by barely three minutes of sound, the successful formula for a sixties pop song. The unorthodox juxtaposition of a baritone singer and a forty piece orchestra combining to score monumental pop hits seemed to be as incongruous as it was short-lived. But after the Walker Brothers' demise in 1967, Scott employed the same musical tactics on his suite of innovative solo albums. Even if the material has grown more complex, then the arrangements retain their sense of awesome magnitude. And the voice in its aspirations is always about to reach for the stars. Walker's interpretation of "Angelica", on *Scott*, a song little discussed by his critics is one of his finest vocal takes, and exemplifies romantic mastery of the ballad. A song of broken-hearted longing in which the protagonist is made to reflect on his mistakes, Walker invokes the lost Angelica as though he is searching for her through the labyrinthine alleys of Venice. This is singing that is unsurpassed of its kind, and one in which the resonant loneliness of the voice creates a new way of addressing unrequited love. Walker's natural method is to foreground romanticism, and to use it as the unashamed principle on which the song is structured. For Sinatra, the romance within a song is coloured by his use of nuance and inflection, and it is almost never the dominant he takes up to bring the song home. Walker and Almond are the first operatic pop singers, in that within their respective limitations of voice they employ the coloratura of the greater medium. Walker's total commitment of voice in songs like "Montague Terrace In Blue", "The Amorous Humphrey Plugg" and "My Death" finds its only parallel in Almond's bravura apparent on numbers like "You Have", "The Stars We Are", "The Slave" and "A Man". At his most successful Almond continues to vitalize a medium begun by the older singer, while elsewhere he is torchier than Scott and more camply theatrical in his delivery.

What is most valuable in creative expression is usually uncategorizable, and belongs to the edge. There have been no shortage of good singers influenced by Sinatra, and amongst them we should include Johnny Mathis and Matt Monro, but male torch singers are a rare breed, with Almond remaining the only British exponent of an essentially female art form. The argument for Walker being Almond's male torch predecessor rests on the strength of Scott's first three solo albums, with their Frenchified influences and cathartically charged emotional singing. But tenderness and compassion too are a part of this register. Walker's sympathies usually remain with the woman's broken heart in the song. His sensitive character-studies of women in songs such as "Mrs. Murphy", "Rosemary", "Big Louise" and "Genevieve", and the compassionate way in which he sympathizes with how women respond to loss are the psychological components that link him to torch song. He doesn't like Almond sing from a woman's point of view, but his empathy with ways in which women suffer contributed to the early image of Scott's ambivalent sexuality.

Sinatra's career may be seen as an attempt to preserve the music of the great modern songwriters, a task that aided by Nelson Riddle's subtle arrangements, he has succeeded in doing. In his fine study of contemporary singers *Jazz Singing*, Will Friedwald expresses a sentiment about the intended durability of Sinatra's work, which seems to pinpoint the singer's intentions. Friedwald writes: "More important than even his conception and perfection of the swingin', lover style, the dominant idiom of non-rock pop singing since the fifties, Sinatra sang and thought in long form, deliberately seeking to create music that would outlive him."

The almost conscious acceptance that his voice will be recognized by posterity is very much part of the assumed Sinatra arrogance, and the way he sits so well with song. And if you can only be imitated and not bettered, then an art form may become too fixed or fluent, and arguably the ability to have put some of the chaos of his life experience into words, would have provided more tension in Sinatra's oeuvre.

Neither Walker nor Almond are pretenders to *bel canto*, and if anything the former has worked to deconstruct the natural facility he possessed for this particular expression of song. Scott professed himself bored with his facile interpretative successes like "Joanna" and "The Lights Of Cincinnati", and was far more at ease pushing Jacques Brel's dissolute character-sketch "Jackie" into the charts, on the tail of its having been banned from radio play on account of offensive lyrics. Walker and Almond have both been the subjects of media censorship, in the way that Baudelaire and Flaubert were both prosecuted by obscenity courts for writing that was thought to be scandalous in *Les Fleurs Du Mal* and *Madame Bovary*. Some of Almond's most richly inventive singles, songs like "Ruby Red" and "Mother Fist" have fallen prey to a censorship unable to separate poetic lyricism from its degrading counterpart, prosaic pornography. It would be inconceivable to think of Sinatra risking lyrics that were not a part of accepted good taste.

I imagine that both Walker and Almond would argue that any expression of inner or self-truth is likely to risk sounding controversial. Both have their origins in a sixties and seventies generation of pop musicians who used music as a subversive weapon to undermine the then pervading socio-sexual ethos. Taboos were broken by sixties pop music, and something of that challenging thrust to tradition is incorporated into the angular dynamic of the two singers under discussion. Both could have become the cabaret artists or crooners that the Sinatra generation saw as their legitimate milieu, but neither has pursued the possibility as a commercial option. Instead, each has sought to diversify, and to live within a metamorphic world of musical changes. Almond oscillates between devotion to the torch ballad and affiliation to dance music, while the hermeticism of Walker's last two albums suggests that he is moving more towards the experimentation of modern classical musicians, and has come to use his voice as a neutral instrument, rather than as a declarative vehicle of romanticism.

Almond's unusual role in male singing has something of the extraordinary about it, which touches on aspects of Shirley Bassey's dominant command amongst female torch singers. His camp theatricality and unashamed willingness to portray vulnerability and hurt in the male, finds a corresponding parallel in Bassey's use of song to compensate for the vicissitudes of love. But Almond hasn't to date allowed himself to become as committed to one genre as Bassey, although he will probably settle to his role as he grows older.

Pop singers of Walker's and Almond's category have a difficult time, in commercially justifying themselves to a corporate record industry. They are cult artists who lack mainstream appeal. Progressively marginalized, they have each negotiated ways of survival, Walker through the legendary status of his past, and Almond by seeking opportunist hits to allow for fan-base-only albums. And although still revered by rock reviewers, and upheld by an older generation who have remained loyal to him from the start of his career, Walker has distanced himself from his pop roots by cultivating obscurity and basing his melodies on the sort of technological disarrangements that have become an integral aesthetic to Brian Eno. Walker's use of scrambled lyrics and deconstructed compositions has something in common with the innovative aspects of David Bowie's Berlin period in the seventies, and with the latter's return to an Eno collaborative deconstructionism on *Outside* (1996). Walker's musical career describes a trajectory from romanticism to postmodernism.

In the 1992 concert programme to his Royal Albert Hall appearance, Marc Almond is described as a "traditional singer", someone at home with the ballad form, but equally capable of performing torch songs to electronic music. In this respect his chosen polarities have never changed, and he's still as likely to come up with a slab of gay disco arrangement, as he is a string orchestrated ballad. If Walker has for personal reasons performed a disappearing act, enforcing his natural propensities for reclusion with a twenty years absence from the stage, then Almond if he is to retain a place in pop is forced to foreground himself in public consciousness. In that way he remains an undefeated romantic, even if the bridge that supports him from the fuming abyss roaring below is a precariously thin one. Almond feels the necessity to challenge the pop charts, but like Walker he may at some stage concede on that issue, and elect instead to record material more concentratedly in harmony with the poetic side of his sensibility.

Sinatra, rather than diversify into mediocre eclecticism, has remained true to swing, the music form that best suits his voice. He is a realist as opposed to a romantic, and part of his credibility as a singer is that he appears to be talking to you direct. Whatever the various moods explored on albums as different as *Songs For Young Lovers, In The Wee Small Hours* or *Only The Lonely*, all from the fifties period of Sinatra's career, the homogenous feel of the singing, whether it is wistfully romantic or tending towards film-noir resignation is always one of plausibility. Nobody is going to doubt what Frank relates, or that he is a feeling-singer given to grounding the emotion in his songs. The sense of disillusionment or world-weariness that he imparts to his tone, is all part of Sinatra's image of somebody for whom love no longer holds any secrets. He has seen through it all. Affairs create the same cyclical consortium of problems, and Frank has articulated most of the joys, doubts, uncertainties, pleasures and pains of heterosexual relationships in the course of half a century of singing.

Almond's emotional trajectory in song entails considerably greater risk. He is often perceived as a gay artist who may take homosexual love as his theme, and is therefore someone unlikely to conform to a Las Vegas repertoire. His unconventionality is his strength, but it entails the necessary sacrifice of large scale popularity.

Walker too in his reaction to *bel canto* has gone for limited popularity in favour of maximum integrity. Admirers of the voice as something distinct from the man, tend to see Walker's career as one of wasted opportunities in which personal neuroses have prevailed over a remarkable talent. Appearing to have become ordained to increasingly longer periods of silence, Walker has grown to represent speculative potential rather than realized projects. The great resonance of the voice is kept on imperturbable hold. What we largely hear are his recordings from the past time-jumped into the present. His voice has alerted the sixties, seventies, eighties and nine-ties to its original romantic structure, without appearing to belong to any of them. Over a long period of time the recorded voice grows to sound disembodied or even posthumous. "Make It Easy On Yourself" is likely to catch you out somewhere in public, its displacement in time almost overwhelming as Scott's baritone emphasis forces the song to improbable reaches. And for those of us who were aware of the song's original release, its survival as something always immediate to the listener provokes a whole series of memory associations concerned with a past compressed into the time duration of the song.

Whatever the merits and defects of his mode of singing Sinatra has stayed on top of the musical world, and held to that pyramidal summit no matter the arrivals and departures of pop acts as big as Elvis Presley, the Beatles and the Rolling Stones. Uncontested in his own generic mode of singing, Sinatra's voice imprint is possibly the most indelible of the last half century. Without an heir to his title, his legacy lies in the continuity of his vast recorded archives. Late night reflections on the flipside of our lives, and the rainy blue aspects of how we perceive love, will always make Sinatra's music indispensable. He and Billie Holiday will continue to companion our solitude on those Sundays when we stand at a high window overlooking the city, and attempt to correlate the emptiness of the thin blue sky with the vacuum we feel in our lives.

Like books, records go out of print, disappear for however long it takes a reputation to be critically reappraised, and then resurface. Scott Walker's solo output lay dormant for twenty years before Fontana re-released the major albums on CD in 1992. In this respect Scott's silence had been absolute. There was no new work, and the legendary albums from his past were unavailable. But somehow the achievement was never forgotten, and I suspect that both Walker and Almond will always occupy a place in the history of romantic pop singing. Their work exists independent of chart popularity, and has come to describe a cultural aesthetic more readily identifiable with French *chanson*, and with the enduring qualities of the best torch, jazz and pop singers.

If Walker's voice initially created a role for the romantic hero, then it's in this vocal cast that he's remembered. The modification of that style to suit his harrowingly intense and lyrically abstruse later albums is a creative transformation known to a smaller cult. In the collective memory Scott will always be situated within the space of the big ballad, no matter that he has disowned his allegiance to this dramatic form. He is the progenitor of a way of singing, that while it clearly separates itself from the style made popular by Sinatra, is nonetheless within the parameters defined by traditional singing. Almond's work has modified the position again. By deliberately testing romanticism on the pop charts through ballad and dance expressions, he has chosen to subvert the latter medium's basic simplicity by contrasting it with finely executed vocals. He has also given us superbly empathetic renditions of songs from the major writers of French *chanson*: Jacques Brel, Leo Ferré and Charles Aznavour. The two albums *Jacques* (1989) and *Absinthe* (1993) find

Almond developing a sensitive tenor's range, and an ability to use short and extended notes on diverse and complex material.

It seems unlikely that Walker will reaccommodate the romantic idiom to his future style of singing. He is like someone who has set fire to a house and walked away from the charred ruins to embrace a new anonymous identity. Almond has lit a torch from the embers, and his cult assemble whenever he pulls the brand from his heart and exposes its heady flame. The romantic agony was how Mario Praz termed the dynamic behind those writers who dedicated themselves to a self-destructive inner truth. Walker either didn't want it, or was unable to sustain his quest for the romantic ideal. Almond still dances amongst the flames, willing again to commit himself to the heroic gesture. "Remember the hero returns" Rilke wrote in the first of his Duino elegies, and we who listen to the voice, await Walker's next musical incarnation.

ENDGAMING

Scott Walker's "Tilt"

What do legends do in their periods of being away? I mean did Lautréamont, the author of *Maldoror* really die on the 24th November 1870 in a modest hotel, 7 Faubourg-Montmartre? Was it really the twenty-three year old body of a mad genius, the prototypical *poète maudit*, who was found dead of unspecified causes on that hotel bed? Or was the real Lautréamont, or Isidore Ducasse drinking in a bar in another quarter of the city, glad of the trick he had played on posterity, and about to take up an anonymous life as a drag artist? We'll never know. History is a continuous fiction, and its inventions afford us access-points to time. *Maldoror* happened in 1868 as an event in Lautréamont's biology. *Tilt* occurred in 1996 after Scott Walker's having been absent from recording for a period of thirteen years. Walker had been presumed dead, mad, or simply dysfunctional by the few who speculated on the reasons behind his absence. An absence that entailed absolute silence.

If Lautréamont walked away from his work, thereby relinquishing responsibility for it, and leaving *Maldoror* to find eventual acclaim by the underground, then Walker's relationship to his own work has formed a similar pattern. Scott indicates from time to time that his voice is still unimpaired, and exists as the resonant instrument that we've always known it to be, only he's been away. Where does he go? Certainly his life has proved one of the world's best kept secrets. There are no disclosures about his private life, no sightings of his person in bars or cafés. Is he someone else in the decade in which he's uncreative? There are no confessional statements from former lovers, or clues from friends as to his whereabouts. The man simply disappears and goes on disappearing. He's always away. And when he returns it's like he's made a transition through the decades with a particular set of songs, and no other biographical evidence to account for his tendency to go missing.

But with the release of his masterpiece *Tilt*, Walker agreed to doing a number of interviews that if anything, only increased the enigma surrounding his private life. Walker, who is really Noel Scott Engel, as Lautréamont was Isidore Ducasse, both appearing pseudonymously to their public, often appears as casual about his material as Lautréamont. "I think I said to you before," he told Richard Cook, "I don't write until I'm ready to record. It's pointless. If I'm going to sit around in a wilderness because I can't record any songs... I threw a whole lot of songs away, as many as I could write. Which isn't a lot. Ever."

Even in conversation Scott Walker puts sunglasses on his words. And in the way that his lyrics have grown to be increasingly minimal, each word afforded the isolation and resonance you would find in a poem by Paul Celan, so his explanations of his work are both obscure and illuminating. Of the tone of the album, and his masterful delivery, Scott comments: "Singing's hard for me. I've always found it difficult, but it's even harder now. I don't mean physically doing it, I mean in the sense of how it sounds, how to make it neutral. Everybody can overload it emotionally or underplay it deadpan, but to get it neutral is very hard, and that's what I'm after. It's an indecision, a grey area of vocal I want to produce."

Walker's manner of addressing a song is usually in the colour spectrum, blue. His insurgent balladic yearning, the authority of his baritone register, and the Spectorish wall of orchestral sound that accompanied his renditions of Bacharach/David tearjerkers were all pitched in a mid-blue to cobalt arena of emotions. Those moody, bluer than blue characteristics of his wounded sensibility only hinted at the increasing isolation that had come to invest Walker's life and work. His retreat has been that of a solitary becoming in time a recluse. And the older Scott grows, the more integral the life and the work appear. This was never a man adopting the role of an outsider, but rather living it and imparting some of that deep pain to his art. Each new album is a co-extension of Scott's telescoping in on his own eventual vanishing-point.

"I shall leave no memoirs," Lautréamont tells us in his short text *Poésies*, a sentiment that I am sure would be endorsed by Walker. *Tilt* would comprise as enigmatic an autobiography as *Poésies*. Walker was prepared to offer us abstruse guidelines as to how his album came into being, but omitted all reference as to why he had been compelled to write it. But even learning of his method is a disclosure we value. "By the time I get to the studio," he tells us, "it's all written down. I have to have musicians I can work with, because I always want the music to be played together, at once. I don't want any drum machines or click tracks. Nothing like that. Very little overdubbing, if possible... I'll do a couple of tunes on the first day, then take them home and listen to them in the evening, go in and do them again If I don't like them – I don't have any equipment at home except a guitar and an amp and a little five-octave keyboard, so I don't have any fantasy or idea of what it'll be like when I get in there. So I'm surprised, constantly."

Who are Scott Walker's neighbours? Does anyone see him come back from a rare visit to the studio? Does anyone hear the demo tapes as he plays them in his flat? Is this all done as an act of ritual secrecy? Lautréamont, we're led to believe, had red hair. Did Isidore Ducasse dye his hair red? What I find so interesting about Scott Walker is the way the enigmatic person behind the work translates so directly into the hermetic qualities of *Tilt*, so that there's no slightest overlap to indicate anything about the artist's private life. Certainly the intensity of the recording, and the harrowing allusions in the songs to war, alienation, and a postmodern landscape from which human relations are absent, suggests the territory explored is about as close to Beckett's endgaming theatre as modern music will get. Walker has shifted his psychological terrain from subjective melancholy to universal anguish.

Scott's obsessive fear of death, or the end, something that has inveterately thumbstained his work to date, was a theme on which he was willing to speak in relation to *Tilt*. "I don't think I've left that behind. I think I'm further into it. I felt it when I was younger in a very vertiginous kind of way, but this time it's more reconciliation, a weightier thing. I realised all the phenomena of existence very young and it was a very hard thing for me. Now I'm living with it a little easier, more as an astonishment thing than a negative thing."

Astonishment perhaps, at the realization of his being fifty-two at the time of recording *Tilt*, as opposed to forty when he recorded its equally hermetic predecessor *Climate Of Hunter*. And few singers have rejected fame in the way that Walker chose to turn his back on considerable pop successes in the mid to late sixties, and elected instead to direct his creative energies towards constructing a music every bit as innovative as the experimental genres established by the likes of Steve Reich, Philip Glass, Terry Riley and Brian Eno. And if the comparison seems incongruous, then I make the analogy in the light of Walker's voice having become an instrument, as we may think of Billie Holiday's voice as an instrument assimilated by her jazz accompanists.

Walker's inimitable, vibrato-drenched baritone scale of singing is used to less effect on *Tilt*, and in its place he seems to have opted for a sonorous tenor's pitch, as a means of best conveying a neutral tone of singing. But there are breathtaking moments on "Patriot (A Single)", where the voice reaches heroic proportions, the operatic thrust sounding as though Scott is keeping in check an energy that is too big to manage. And the arias that he constructs in these brief, but dramatic vocal cameos in "Patriot (A Single)" are composed around allusions to South American torturers, as in the song "Bolivia". "The bad news/is there is I no news" he affirms, before the voice spectacularly alludes to the story of a deserter: "Tonight he'll/rise/he'll leave/these arms/to anyone/who asks/about/as-in-the tracks/as-in-the wrists/I as-in-you been/as-in-without." Walker would doubtless claim that the fragmentation and obscurity of the lyrics are a part of his attempt to find in songwriting the visual equivalents of film. Incidents in the scrambled narratives that comprise the songs on *Tilt* flash by, seemingly unrelated, but somehow forming an articulate and integrated texture in the overall composition. Scott's method of writing has always tended towards the neologistic and the grammatically angular, and his emphasis tends to lie on phrases that convey a poetic rather than literal meaning. In this particular set of lyrics he talks about having stripped the constituents of lyric to their bare components. The words in *Tilt* are horribly isolated, like prisoners awaiting torture in a concentration camp. The singer can't protect his delivery, the words he has written return on his voice with a renewed sense of vulnerability, and the timeless process imparted to them by recording means they will remain exposed at every new listening.

What is it that has Walker concern himself in these transpersonal songs with themes arising from South American torturers, Nazi war criminals like Eichmann, and the death of the Italian film director Pier Paolo Pasolini? Or do these characters represent symbolic personae brought in to enforce the devastated inner landscape that Scott inhabits? There are no autobiographical confessions on *Tilt*, and no least traces of self-pity, there is only the unrelenting disquiet of genius that has somewhere along the line been broken.

Edmundo Montagne had been a childhood friend of Isidore Ducasse's in Montevideo, that is before Ducasse left for Paris and assumed the name Comte de Lautréamont. In an article he wrote in 1925, Montagne who kept in touch with Isidore's father, expressed something of the mystery surrounding the young poet's death. "I heard no mention of the *Chants*, neither then or when I grew up. All Francois Ducasse told me, one day, post-1875, was that Isidore had died in '70. I had always thought he'd been killed in the war."

The mystery investing Isidore Ducasse's life and death give him the appeal of a perverse saint. We know little of how he lived, and even less of how he died. In a way, he's the perfect subject for a Scott Walker song, for the two mirror each other in terms of biographical obscurity. Who was Isidore Ducasse? Who is Scott Walker? Is the latter a reincarnation of the former? Have either of them ever existed independent of the work they have given us?

The dilemma on which Scott's career has foundered is a peculiarly modern one for singers. Walker's rise to fame in the sixties was as part of a generation which called itself singer/songwriters, and who largely discredited vocalists who interpreted material written for them. That being a singer does not necessarily imply an ability to write lyrics was seen as no impediment to a new generation of pop musicians. Walker who had begun his career as an interpretative artist would normally have stayed in the tradition of a long line of singers whose gift was their voice, and whose creativity was measured by their individual genius in colouring the lyrics. Anxious to explore his own anxiety-driven inner world, Scott inspired by the poetic lyricism of the Belgian songwriter Jacques Brel, took to interspersing songs written by the latter with self-penned compositions on his first three solo albums. *Scott 4* was entirely self-composed, and *Til The Band Comes In* comprised half cover versions, and half Walker material. After that, Walker appears to have lost confidence in his songwriting abilities, and his next four solo albums all featured him in the role of interpreting covers. And so the conflict raged right through the Walker Brothers reunion in the late seventies, until Scott's re-emergence with the masterful, self-written *Climate Of Hunter* in 1984.

But it's an agony that's little talked about. Opera singers are not required to compose librettos, and so why are gifted vocalists like Scott Walker expected to write original material? Isn't the voice sufficient as a creative instrument? Billie Holiday, Sarah Vaughan, Dusty Springfield, Peggy Lee, Shirley Bassey, Elvis Presley, Gene Pitney and Roy Orbison are all examples of singers who have relied on songwriting teams to tailor lyric and melody to their individual voices.

In Walker's case, self-composition, while it has greatly reduced his output as a singer, has allowed him to channel his creative energies into the two recondite suites of songs that comprise *Climate Of Hunter* and *Tilt*. Would we have liked an expansive repertoire of cover versions, with Scott singing Cole Porter, Leiber/Stoller and Charles Aznavour? Marc Almond's impassioned renditions of Aznavour's "Yesterday When I Was Young" and "What Makes A Man A Man", suggests that Scott could equally have applied his vocal prowess to these modern classics. Walker's output, scarcely

---

more than an hour and a half's music in thirteen years, is alarmingly unprolific by any standards. Is it disinterest that accounts for so minimal an output, or it is a perfectionist ideal that fears failure? Is there a lack of momentum due to the artist having renounced his past successes, and with it the public who once bought his records? Lautréamont had almost no readers at the time of his disappearance. In his long periods of creative inertia, Scott addresses the public through periodic compilation releases drawn from the more commercial phases of his work. These selections and *Best Of*s have something of a posthumous air about them. Where is the singer? A blond-haired Scott, photographed twenty-five years ago stares out from the CD racks, enforcing the rumours of a death that hasn't quite happened, except in term of new material. Is there a death-pact between Scott and a bourbon bottle, or has silence become the most cherished aspect of his being? Is Scott listening to the empty space his voice inhabits? Walker's life is as much an open-ended fiction as Lautréamont's. I placed Lautréamont in a drag bar, wearing a red wig and black suspenders. What if that really happened. In my invention Lautréamont who was really Isidore Ducasse became a stripper called Isidore. Isidore or Isidora?

What is Scott doing at this moment? Is he out in Bayswater visiting the local supermarket? Nobody in the street or at the check-out point knows this person as the singer Scott Walker. His cheque card probably reads Noel Scott Engel. Voice is a concealed phenomenon. It's like a flower that opens in response to the sun. Scott's voice seems to be periodically unlocked from its subterranean depths by an inner urgency that progressively grows until it can no longer be restrained. The poet W.B. Yeats once wrote of the incredible resistance he felt to the poetic experience, and how he only wrote the words down after they had come to assert a dominance that forced him to speak them out loud. In other words, the lyric impulse demanded attention. It wanted out.

I suspect Walker's inspirational guidelines operate on similar levels of breakthrough. He creates only when there is no other option, and also as he points out, only when there is someone to finance his uncommercial experiments. Part of Walker's dilemma is how far out of the mainstream can he go and yet still retain a public. His following is loyal, but one suspects that his solid nucleus of admirers have remained with him from the start, and have not come to *Tilt* without previous knowledge of his work. The album is more readily assimilated if we see it as a continuing line in Scott's development as an artist and as an affirmation of the uncompromising integrity he has always brought to his work.

But where are we now in terms of Scott being present as a

singer? In an unlikely interview with Simon Williams for the *NME*, Walker confessed to still being disturbed by an innate sense of self-loathing, but spoke of having come to terms with the negative aspects of his past. With his usual sense of only hinting at his private darkness, he reflected: "Do I feel as though I did anything wrong? No, not through those times. I might have done earlier on, but I can't remember what they were because I was, uh, pretty gone. I can't remember anything. Anyway, they're a waste of time, regrets."

Scott is undoubtedly alluding here to alcoholism, and the years he wrote off through heavy drinking. The reported earlier mismanaged suicide attempts, followed by a brief and failed marriage to Mette Teglbjaerg, seem to have been succeeded by a self-destructive impulse to drink himself into oblivion. According to Plotinus and the neo-Platonists, we forget our previous incarnation at the moment of birth, and then set about retrieving what we once knew through the faculty of memory. Often it is suffering which alerts us to the need to sensitize memory, and having opened the door, we long to close it again in order to forget. Ultimately we die in order to let go the accumulated pain of living. The same phenomenon confronts the creative artist. How much does one dare to remember? And how much forget? Good art finds a balance between the two, and we call it remembering.

Where is Scott in this process of retrieval? *Tilt* seemed like a refusal to incorporate autobiography into the lyric texture, but hopefully the internal pressures of growing older may inspire him to record a successor to *Tilt*. "I wouldn't write," he explained, endeavouring to account for the lost years, "because there was this thing whereby you had to make demos, and I can't imagine demoing any of my material. The idea is totally ridiculous. So I simply took years off."

I imagine no-one will ever penetrate Walker's veneer, and that like Lautréamont his life will remain an insoluble mystery. If by some weird trick of time we could bring the two together, the red-haired youth who died for his art, and perversely denied us the promise of genius, and the young man who turned away from fulfilment as a singer, would they share a moment's understanding? Lautréamont used to walk through the Paris streets looking for something or someone, presumably himself. Scott is probably doing the same this moment. Walking head down, thinking, threading the streets of Bayswater and Queensway. The past is behind him like the indifferent indigo rain-sky building over Hyde Park. He doesn't even look up at the clouds roofing the city. He's headed towards something called the future, which is always now. The next station of the cross is an off-licence, and then back home. He closes the door and faces himself. Recollection is blue on blue. Who are you Scott Walker?

SELECTIVE DISCOGRAPHY

This selective discography spans Scott Walker's recorded musical career from the start of The Walker Brothers to the present day. No claim is being made that the discography is definitive.

Information relates mainly to British releases, and no attempt has been made to cover US/foreign releases in any depth. Such information is outside the scope of this present book but may form part of a future edition.

If there are any inaccuracies or omissions or you have any additional information then please contact Walkerpeople, the official Scott Walker fan club, whose address is at the back of this book.

This discography has been compiled from information kindly supplied by Lynne Goodall from Walkerpeople.

WALKER BROTHERS
British Singles:

Pretty Girls Everywhere/Doin' The Jerk – *Philips BF 1401* (1964)

Love Her/The Seventh Dawn – *Philips BF 1409* (1965)

Make It Easy On Yourself/But I Do – *Philips BF 1428* (1965)

My Ship Is Coming In/You're All Around Me – *Philips BF 1454* (1965)

The Sun Ain't Gonna Shine Anymore/After The Lights Go Out – *Philips BF 1473* (1966)

(Baby) You Don't Have To Tell Me/My Love Is Growing – *Philips BF 1497* (1966)

Another Tear Falls/Saddest Night In The World – *Philips BF 1514* (1966)

Deadlier Than The Male/Archangel – *Philips BF 1537* (1966)

Stay With Me Baby/Turn Out The Moon – *Philips BF 1548* (1967)

Walking In The Rain/Baby Make It The Last Time – *Philips BF 1576* (1967)

No Regrets/Remember Me – *GTO GT 42* (1975)

Lines/First Day – *GTO GT 67* (1976)

We're All Alone/Have You Seen My Baby – *GTO GT 78* (1976)

The Electrician/Den Haague – *GTO GT 230* (1978)

First Love Never Dies/The Sun Ain't Gonna Shine Anymore – *Phonogram IPS 001* (1982)

The Sun Ain't Gonna Shine Anymore/In My Room – *Bam Caruso OPRA 090* (1987) (Limited edition single from *Live In Japan* reissue album)

WALKER BROTHERS/SCOTT WALKER

British singles:

The Sun Ain't Gonna Shine Anymore/Jackie – *Fontana (UK) WALK RI: (INT) 866372-7* (1991) [reissue]
The Sun Ain't Gonna Shine Anymore/First Love Never Dies/Jackie/Joanna – *Fontana (UK) WALK R112: (INT) 866373-1* (1991) [12" single – reissue]
The Sun Ain't Gonna Shine Anymore/Jackie – *Fontana (UK) WALK MI: (INT) 866372-4* (1991) [cassette single – reissue]
No Regrets/Boy Child – *Fontana (UK) WALKR – 2: (INT) 866 600-7* (1992) [reissue]
No Regrets/Boy Child – *Fontana (UK) WALKM – 2: (INT) 866 600-4* (1992) [cassette single – reissue]

Maxi singles:

Love Her/The Sun Ain't Gonna Shine Anymore/Make It Easy On Yourself – *Philips 6051 017* (1971)
The Sun Ain't Gonna Shine Anymore/Make It Easy On Yourself/Stay With Me Baby – *Philips 6160 050* (1976)
Make It Easy On Yourself/The Sun Ain't Gonna Shine Anymore/My Ship Is Coming In *Philips Classic Cuts series* (1980)

British E.P.s:

"I Need You": Looking For Me/Young Man Cried/Everything's Gonna Be Alright/I Need You – *Philips BE 12596* (1966)
"Solo Scott, Solo John": Sunny/Come Rain Or Come Shine/The Gentle Rain/Mrs Murphy – *Philips BE 12597* (1966)
"Hits Of The Walker Brothers": Another Tear Falls/Summertime/The Sun Ain't Gonna Shine Anymore/Make It Easy On Yourself – *Philips MCP-1002* (1967) [cassette-only compilation]
"Hits Of The Walker Bros & Dusty Springfield": (2 tracks by The Walker Bros. & 2 by Dusty – track titles unknown) – *Philips MC* (1967) [cassette only compilation]
"The Walker Brothers EP": Shutout/The Electrician/Nite Flights/Fat Mama Kick – *GTO GT 295* (1981)

WALKER BROTHERS

British L.P.s:

Take It Easy With The Walker Brothers: *Philips BL 7691* (1965)
Make It Easy On Yourself/There Goes My Baby/First Love Never Dies/Dancing In The Street/Lonely Winds/The Girl I Lost In The Rain/Land Of 1000 Dances/You're All Around Me/Love Minus Zero (No Limit)/I Don't Want To Hear It Anymore/Here Comes The Night/Tell The Truth.

Portrait: *Philips BL 7732* (1966)
In My Room/Saturday's Child/Just For A Thrill/Hurting Each Other/Old Folks/Summertime/People Get Ready/I Can See It Now/Where's The Girl/Living Above Your Head/Take It Like A Man/No Sad Songs For Me.

Images: *Philips BL 7770* (1967)
Everything Under The Sun/Once Upon A Summertime/Experience/Blueberry Hill/Orpheus/Stand By Me/I Wanna Know/I Will Wait For You/It Makes No Difference Now/I Can't Let It Happen To You/Genevieve/Just Say Goodbye.

No Regrets: *GTO GTLP 007* (1975)
No Regrets [Scott solo version]/Hold An Old Friend's Hand/Boulder To Birmingham/Walking In The Sun/Lover's Lullaby/Got To Have You/He'll Break Your Heart/Everything That Touches You/Lovers/Burn Our Bridges.

Lines: *GTO GTLP 014* (1976)
Lines/Taking It All In Stride/Inside Of You/Have You Seen My Baby/We're All Alone/Many Rivers To Cross/First Day/Brand New Tennessee Waltz/Hard To Be Friends/Dreaming As One.

Nite Flights: *GTO GTLP 033* (1978)
Shutout/Fat Mama Kick/Nite Flights/The Electrician/Death Of Romance/Den Haague/Rhythms Of Vision/Disciples Of Death/Fury And The Fire/Child Of Flames.

The Walker Brothers Live in Japan: *Bam Caruso AIDA 076* (1987) [double album, previously issued 1968 – only in Japan]
Land Of 1000 Dances/I Need You/Everything

Under The Sun/Tell Me How Do You Feel/ Watch Your Step/Uptight/In My Room/The Lady Came From Baltimore/Living Above Your Head/Dizzie Miss Lizzie/Twinkie-Lee/ Hold On I'm Coming/Annabella/Yesterday/ Reach Out I'll Be There/Make It Easy On Yourself/Saturday's Child/Walking In The Rain/The Sun Ain't Gonna Shine Anymore/ Turn On Your Lovelight/Ooh Poo Pah Doo [+ Scott's thanks to musicians/ Walkers' message taken from their *Images* album and only previously available on the Japanese release of the album]

British Compilation L.P.s:
The Walker Brothers Story: *Philips DBLOO2A/B* (1967) [double album]
Make It Easy On Yourself/Land Of 1000 Dances/Young Man Cried/Living Above Your Head/I Need You/My Ship Is Coming In/ Saturday's Child/Mrs Murphy/The Sun Ain't Gonna Shine Anymore/Just For A Thrill/ Summertime/In My Room/Stand By Me/Once Upon A Summertime/Experience/Come Rain Or Come Shine/Archangel/People Get Ready/ Stay With Me Baby/Genevieve/Walking In The Rain/I Wanna Know/Just Say Goodbye.

The Fabulous Walker Brothers: *Wing WLII88* (Re-released on *Fontana FLI3078*)
There Goes My Baby/First Love Never Dies/ Sunny/Come Rain Or Come Shine/Looking For Me/Deadlier Than The Male/Saturday's Child/Young Man Cried/The Gentle Rain/Mrs Murphy/Everything's Gonna Be Alright/After The Lights Go Out.

The Immortal Walker Brothers: *Contour 6870 564* (Re-released as *The Walker Brothers: Make It Easy On Yourself – Contour CN2017*)
Make It Easy On Yourself/Dancing In The Street/Land Of 1000 Dances/Here Comes The Night/In My Room/Just For A Thrill/I Can See It Now/Living Above Your Head/ Everything Under The Sun/Genevieve.

The Walker Brothers: Make It Easy On Yourself: *Philips International 6336 214*
Make It Easy On Yourself/Land Of 1000 Dances/My Ship Is Coming In/The Sun Ain't Gonna Shine Anymore/Love Minus Zero (No

Limit)/Dancing In The Street/Here Comes The Night/Once Upon A Summertime/Saturday's Child/I Will Wait For You/Orpheus/Stand By Me.

The Walker Brothers: Greatest Hits: *Philips International Double Album 6640 009*
Land Of 1000 Dances/Make It Easy On Yourself/There Goes My Baby/Everything Under The Sun/People Get Ready/Pretty Girls Everywhere/I Don't Want To Hear It Anymore/The Sun Ain't Gonna Shine Anymore/Stay With Me Baby/Saturday's Child/First Love Never Dies/I Wanna Know/ Doin' The Jerk/My Ship Is Coming In/Dancing In The Street/Love Her/Hurting Each Other/ Love Minus Zero (No Limit)/Lonely Winds/ The Seventh Dawn/Tell The Truth/(Baby) You Don't Have To Tell Me/Stand By Me/ Everything's Gonna Be Alright/I Need You/ Another Tear Falls/Walking In The Rain/Just Say Goodbye.

Spotlight On The Walker Brothers: *Philips International Double Album 6640 013*
The Sun Ain't Gonna Shine Anymore/My Love Is Growing/No Sad Songs For Me/Turn Out The Moon/Old Folks/In My Room/Living Above Your Head/Make It Easy On Yourself/ Young Man Cried/Saddest Night In The World/Deadlier Than The Male/Genevieve/My Ship Is Coming In/It Makes No Difference Now/Here Comes The Night/The Girl I Lost In The Rain/Orpheus/Once Upon A Summertime/You're All Around Me/I Can See It Now/Where's The Girl/Mrs Murphy/ Archangel/Experience.

Pop Lions: The Sun Ain't Gonna Shine Anymore: *Fontana 6430 152*
The Sun Ain't Gonna Shine Anymore/You're All Around Me/Land Of 1000 Dances/Take It Like A Man/Baby Make It The Last Time/ Walking In The Rain/(Baby) You Don't Have To Tell Me/My Love Is Growing/Turn Out The Moon/Deadlier Than The Male/Make It Easy On Yourself/I Can't Let It Happen To You.

The Best Of The Walker Brothers: *Philips Sonic Series 7175 500* [cassette only]
The Sun Ain't Gonna Shine Anymore/Make It Easy On Yourself/I Don't Want To Hear It

Anymore/Tell The Truth/Lonely Winds/Love Minus Zero (No Limit)/My Ship Is Coming In/Land Of 1000 Dances/You're All Around Me/There Goes My Baby/Here Comes The Night/First Love Never Dies.

Walker Brothers' Hits: *Phonogram 6463 139* (1982)
Make It Easy On Yourself/Love Her/My Ship Is Coming In/Dancing In The Street/The Sun Ain't Gonna Shine Anymore/Land Of 1000 Dances/(Baby) You Don't Have To Tell Me/Another Tear Falls/Deadlier Than The Male/Stand By Me/Walking In The Rain/Stay With Me Baby.

The Walker Brothers: Music For The Millions: *Fontana 812-345-1*
The Sun Ain't Gonna Shine Anymore/Make It Easy On Yourself/There Goes My Baby/My Ship Is Coming In/Land Of 1000 Dances/Here Comes The Night/In My Room/Living Above Your Head/I Need You/No Sad Songs For Me/Stay With Me Baby/Summertime.

The Walker Bros: After The Lights Go Out – The Best Of 1965–67: *Fontana 842831-1* (1990) Love Her/Make It Easy On Yourself/First Love Never Dies/Deadlier Than The Male/Another Tear Falls/After The Lights Go Out/Mrs Murphy/In My Room/Archangel/The Sun Ain't Gonna Shine Anymore/Saddest Night In The World/Young Man Cried/Stay With Me Baby/Orpheus/I Can't Let It Happen To You/Just Say Goodbye.

WALKER BROTHERS/SCOTT WALKER

British L.P.s:
No Regrets: The Best Of Scott Walker And The Walker Brothers 1965–1976: *Fontana 510 831-1* (1992)
No Regrets/Make It Easy On Yourself/The Sun Ain't Gonna Shine Anymore/My Ship Is Coming In/Joanna/Lights Of Cincinnati/Another Tear Falls/Boy Child/Montague Terrace (In Blue)/Jackie/Stay With Me Baby/If You Go Away/First Love Never Dies/Love Her/Walking In The Rain/(Baby) You Don't Have To Tell Me/Deadlier Than The Male/We're All Alone. [Cassette *510 831-4*]

SCOTT WALKER

Singles:
Jackie/The Plague (UK) *Philips 1628* (1967)
Jackie/Wait Until Dark (Denmark) *Philips 326 852 BF*
Amsterdam/Mathilde (Spain) *Philips 326 859 BF*
Joanna/Always Coming Back To You (UK) *Philips 1662* (1968)
Joanna/Always Coming Back To You (Holland) *Philips 326 876 BF*
Joanna/Always Coming Back To You (Spain) *Philips 326 876 BF*
The Rope And The Colt/Concerto Pour Guitar (France) *Philips B.370780 F* (1968)
Lights Of Cincinnati/Two Weeks Since You've Gone (UK) *Philips 1793* (1969)
Lights Of Cincinnati/Two Weeks Since You've Gone (USA) *Smash 2228*
Lights Of Cincinnati/Two Weeks Since You've Gone (Germany) *Philips 326 981 BF*
Lights Of Cincinnati
(S. Africa) *Philips 561*
Til The Band Comes In/Jean The Machine (Holland) *Philips 6006 107* (1970)
I Still See You/My Way Home (UK) *Philips 6006 168* (1971)
The Me I Never Knew/This Way Mary (UK) *Philips 6006 311* (1973)
A Woman Left Lonely/Where Love Has Died (UK) *CBS 1795* (1973)
A Woman Left Lonely/Where Love Has Died (Holland) *CBS 1795*
Delta Dawn/We Had It All (UK) *CBS 2521* (1974)
Track 3/Blanket Roll Blues (UK) *Virgin VS 666* (1984)
Man From Reno/Indecent Sacrifice (France) *Fontana CD 862 382-2* (1993) [Cassette *862 382-4*]

E.P.s:
Mathilde/Amsterdam/The Lady Came From Baltimore/Angelica (Yugoslavia) – *Philips 532260* (1967)
Mathilde/Montague Terrace (In Blue)/Angelica/When Joanna Loved Me (France) – *Philips 438-4021* (1967)
"Great Scott": *Philips MCP-1006* (1967) [cassette only]
Jackie/When Joanna Loved Me/The Plague/Mathilde

L.P.s:

Looking Back With Scott Walker: (UK) – *Ember 3393* (1967) [recorded 1958/9]
Too Young/I Don't Want To Know/Comin' Home/Bluebell/Paper Doll/Sunday/When I Kiss You Goodnight/Sing Boy Sing/Too Young To Know/Take This Love/Till You Return/When You See Her/All I Do Is Dream Of You/ Everybody But Me.

Scott: (UK) – *Philips 7816* (1967)
[Also on (USA) – *Smash 7099* – under the title of *Aloner* and released 1968]
Mathilde/Montague Terrace (In Blue)/ Angelica/The Lady Came From Baltimore/ When Joanna Loved Me/My Death/The Big Hurt/Such A Small Love/Through A Long And Sleepless Night/You're Gonna Hear From Me/Always Coming Back To You/ Amsterdam.

Scott 2 (UK) – *Philips 7840* (1968)
[Also on (USA) – *Smash 7106*, 1968]
Jackie/Best Of Both Worlds/The Amorous Humphrey Plugg/Black Sheep Boy/Next/The Girls From The Streets/Plastic Palace People/ Wait Until Dark/The Girls And The Dogs/ Windows Of The World/The Bridge/Come Next Spring.

Scott 3: (UK) – *Philips 7882* (1969)
[Also on (USA) *Smash 7121*, 1969. The Smash release has the track "Lights Of Cincinnati" in place of "30 Century Man"]
It's Raining Today/Copenhagen/Rosemary/Big Louise/We Came Through/Butterfly/Two Ragged Soldiers/30 Century Man/Winter Night/Two Weeks Since You've Gone/Sons Of/Funeral Tango/If You Go Away.

Scott Sings Songs From His T.V. Series (UK) – *Philips 7900* (1969)
I Have Dreamed/Impossible Dream/Will You Still Be Mine/When The World Was Young/ Who Will Take My Place)/If She Walked Into My Life/The Song Is You/The Look Of Love/ Country Girl/Someone To Light Up My Life/ Only The Young/Lost In The Stars.

(NOEL SCOTT ENGEL)
Scott 4: (UK) – *Philips 7913* (1969)
The Seventh Seal/On Your Own Again/ World's Strongest Man/Angels Of Ashes/Boy Child/The Old Man's Back Again/Hero Of The War/Duchess/Get Behind Me/Rhymes Of Goodbye

Best Of Scott Walker – Vol. 1: (UK) – *Philips 7910* (1970) [reissues]
Joanna/Montague Terrace (In Blue)/Jackie/ Copenhagen/Big Louise/Mathilde/Plastic Palace People/If She Walked Into My Life/ Lady Came From Baltimore/The Impossible Dream.

Til The Band Comes In: (UK) – *Philips 6308 035* (1970)
Prologue/Little Things (That Keep Us Together)/Joe/Thanks For Chicago Mr James/ Long About Now/Time Operator/Jean The Machine/Cowbells Shakin'/Til The Band Comes In/The War Is Over/Stormy/The Hills Of Yesterday/Reuben James/What Are You Doing The Rest Of Your Life/It's Over.

This Is Scott Walker – Vol 1: (UK) – *Philips 6382 007* (1971) [reissues]
Lady Came From Baltimore/When Joanna Loved Me/Amsterdam/Always Coming Back To You/Mathilde/Montague Terrace (In Blue)/ Angelica/Jackie/Best Of Both Worlds/Plastic Palace People/Black Sheep Boy/Copenhagen.

This Is Scott Walker – Vol 2: (UK) – *Philips 6382 052* (1972) [reissues]
Impossible Dream/Windows Of The World/ Come Next Spring/Will You Still Be Mine/ Look Of Love/Lost In The Stars/If You Go Away/Sons Of/Two Ragged Soldiers/It's Raining Today/What Are You Doing The Rest Of Your Life/Til The Band Comes In.

The Moviegoer: (UK) – *Philips 6308 120* (1972) [Also released on the Contour label, with the same track content but different sleeve: *Contour 6870 633*]
This Way Mary/Speak Softly Love/Glory Road/That Night/Summer Of '42/Easy Come Easy Go/Ballad Of Sacco & Vanzetti/Face In The Crowd/Joe Hill/Loss Of Love/All His Children/Come Saturday Morning.

The Best Of Scott Walker: (UK) – *Contour 6870* (1972) [reissues]

Joanna/Speak Softly Love/Summer Of '42/ Copenhagen/Angelica/Jackie/Lights Of Cincinnati/Glory Road/Best Of Both Worlds/ Lady Came From Baltimore/When Joanna Loved Me/Mathilde.

Any Day Now: (UK) – *Philips 6308 148* (1973)
Any Day Now/All My Love's Laughter/Do I Love You/Maria Bethania/Cowboy/When You Get Right Down To It/If/Ain't No Sunshine/ The Me I Never Knew/If Ships Were Made To Sail/We Could Be Flying.

Attention: Scott Walker: (UK) – *Fontana 6438 083* (1973) [reissues]
Jackie/Do I Love You/We Could Be Flying/ Who (Will Take My Place)/Black Sheep Boy/If You Go Away/Joanna/Come Next Spring/ Lights Of Cincinnati/Stormy/Windows Of The World/Get Behind Me.

Stretch: (UK) – *CBS 65725* (1973)
Sunshine/Just One Smile/A Woman Left Lonely/No Easy Way Down/That's How I Got To Memphis/Use Me/Frisco Depot/Someone Who Cared/Where Does Brown Begin/Where Love Has Died/I'll Be Home.

The Romantic Scott Walker: (UK) – *Philips 6850 013* (1973) [reissues]
Will You Still Be Mine/I Have Dreamed/When The World Was Young/Who (Will Take My Place)/Impossible Dream/Mathilde/Montague Terrace (In Blue)/Angelica/My Death/Lady Came From Baltimore/When Joanna Loved Me.

We Had It All: (UK) – *CBS 80254* (1974)
Low Down Freedom/We Had It All/Black Rose/Ride Me Down Easy/You're Young And You'll Forget/The House Song/Whatever Happened To Saturday Night/Sundown/Old Five And Dimers Like Me/Delta Dawn.

Spotlight On Scott Walker: (UK) – *Philips 6625 017* (1976) [Double album: reissues]
Do I Love You/Joanna/Country Girl/Speak Softly Love/I Will Wait For You/Summer Of '42/We Could Be Flying/Who (Will Take My Place)/If/Lost In The Stars/Lights Of Cincinnati/What Are You Doing The Rest Of

Your Life/I Still See You/When Joanna Loved Me/Stormy/Little Things (That Keep Us Together)/Big Louise/Copenhagen/Joe/My Way Home/Butterfly/Get Behind Me/Jackie/ Sons Of/Next/If You Go Away/Mathilde/ Amsterdam/The Girls And The Dogs/Funeral Tango.

Fire Escape In The Sky – The God-Like Genius Of Scott Walker: (UK) – *Zoo 2* (1981) [reissues]
Such A Small Love/Big Louise/Little Things (That Keep Us Together)/Plastic Palace People/The Girls From The Streets/It's Raining Today/The Seventh Seal/The Amorous Humphrey Plugg/Angels Of Ashes/Boy Child/ Montague Terrace (In Blue)/Always Coming Back To You.

Scott Walker Sings Jacques Brel: (UK) – *Phonogram 6359 090* (1981) [reissues]
Jackie/Next/The Girls And The Dogs/If You Go Away/Funeral Tango/Mathilde/ Amsterdam/Sons of/My Death/Little Things (That Keep Us Together).

The Best Of Scott Walker: (UK) – *Phonogram 6381 073* (1982) [reissues]
Joanna/Lights Of Cincinnati/Will You Still Be Mine/I Will Wait For You/Montague Terrace (In Blue)/When Joanna Loved Me/Jackie/The Lady Came From Baltimore/If She Walked Into My Life/The Me I Never Knew/If You Go Away/The Impossible Dream.

Scott Engel – Scott: (UK) – *Philips 7564 002* [cassette only – reissues]
Jackie/Black Sheep Boy/Windows Of The World/The Big Hurt/The Amorous Humphrey Plugg/Rhymes Of Goodbye/Best Of Both Worlds/If You Go Away/Mathilde/Angelica/ The Lady Came From Baltimore/Always Coming Back To You/When Joanna Loved Me/The Old Man's Back Again/Plastic Palace People/Wait Until Dark/Copenhagen/It's Raining Today/Funeral Tango/Montague Terrace (In Blue)/I Have Dreamed/Country Girl/Who (Will Take My Place)/The Impossible Dream.

Climate Of Hunter: (UK) – *Virgin V2303* (1984)

Rawhide/Dealer/Track 3/Sleepwalker's Woman/Track 5/Track 6/Track 7/Blanket Roll Blues.

Boy Child – The Best Of 1967–70: (UK) – *Fontana 842832-1* (1990) [reissues]
The Plague/Montague Terrace (In Blue)/Such A Small Love/The Amorous Humphrey Plugg/Plastic Palace People/The Bridge/Big Louise/We Came Through/The Seventh Seal/Boy Child/The Old Man's Back Again/Prologue/Little Things (That Keep Us Together)/Time Operator.

Tilt: (UK) – *Fontana 526 859-1* [vinyl LP: Limited Edition] (1995)
(USA: *Drag City DC134* [vinyl LP] 1997)
Farmer In The City/The Cockfighter/Bouncer see Bouncer.../Manhattan/Face On Breast/Bolivia '95/Patriot (A Single)/Tilt/Rosary.

Compact Discs
Climate Of Hunter: (UK) *Virgin CD V2303* (1989): Tracks as per above album release.

Boy Child – The Best Of 1967–70 (UK) *Fontana 842832-2* (1990) [reissues]
The Plague/Montague Terrace (In Blue)/Such A Small Love/The Amorous Humphrey Plugg/The Girls From The Streets/Plastic Palace People/The Bridge/It's Raining Today/Copenhagen/Big Louise/We Came Through/The Seventh Seal/On Your Own Again/Boy Child/The Old Man's Back Again/Prologue/Little Things (That Keep Us Together)/Time Operator/The War Is Over (Sleepers)/Epilogue/The Rope And The Colt.

Scott Walker Sings Jacques Brel: (UK) *Fontana 838212-2* (1991) [reissues]
Mathilde/Amsterdam/My Death/Next/The Girls And The Dogs/If You Go Away/Funeral Tango/Sons Of.

Scott: (UK) *Fontana 510 879-2* (1992) [reissue] (Cassette 510 879-4)
Mathilde/Montague Terrace (In Blue)/Angelica/The Lady Came From Baltimore/When Joanna Loved Me/My Death/The Big Hurt/Such A Small Love/You're Gonna Hear From Me/Through A Long And Sleepless Night/Always Coming Back To You/

Amsterdam.

Scott 2: (UK) *Fontana 510 880-2* (1992) [reissue] (Cassette 510 880-4)
Jackie/Best Of Both Worlds/Black Sheep Boy/The Amorous Humphrey Plugg/Next/The Girls From The Streets/Plastic Palace People/Wait Until Dark/The Girls And The Dogs/Windows Of The World/The Bridge/Come Next Spring.

Scott 3: (UK) *Fontana 510 881-2* (1992) [reissue] (Cassette *510 881-4*)
It's Raining Today/Copenhagen/Rosemary/Big Louise/We Came Through/Butterfly/Two Ragged Soldiers/30 Century Man/Winter Night/Two Weeks Since You've Gone/Sons Of/Funeral Tango/If You Go Away.

Scott 4: (UK) *Fontana 510 882-2* (1992) [reissue] (Cassette 510 882-4)
The Seventh Seal/On Your Own Again/The World's Strongest Man/Angels Of Ashes/Boy Child/Hero Of The War/The Old Man's Back Again/Duchess/Get Behind Me/Rhymes Of Goodbye.

Man From Reno (Edit)/Indecent Sacrifice: (France) – *Fontana CD Single 862 382-2* (1993) (Cassette *862 382-04*)

Scott Walker And The Walker Brothers: 1965–1993: (France) *Fontana 518094-2* (1993) [reissues]
Man From Reno [unedited]/The Sun Ain't Gonna Shine Anymore/No Regrets/Make It Easy On Yourself/The Old Man's Back Again/The World's Strongest Man/It's Raining Today/Big Louise/We Came Through/The Seventh Seal/The Girls From The Streets/Plastic Palace People/Montague Terrace (In Blue)/Mathilde/Jackie/Indecent Sacrifice/The Plague/Joanna/The War Is Over. (Cassette *518094-4*: tracks as above, but excluding: The Plague/Joanna/The War Is Over)

Scott Walker And The Walker Brothers: A Very Special Collection: (UK) *Pickwick PWKS 4165* (1993) [reissues] (Cassette *PWK MC 4165*)
No Regrets/Shutout/Lines/We're All Alone/Many Rivers To Cross/Brand New Tennessee Waltz/Nite Flights/Boulder To Birmingham/

Burn Our Bridges/Just One Smile/No Easy Way Down/I'll Be Home/We Had It All/Sundown/Ride Me Down Easy/Delta Dawn.

Looking Back With Scott Walker: (UK) *Fat Boy Records Fat CD 226* (1994) [reissue]
Too Young/I Don't Want To Know/Comin' Home/Bluebell/Paper Doll/Sunday/When I Kiss You Goodnite/Sing Boy Sing/Too Young To Know/Take This Love/Till You Return/When You See Her/All I Do Is Dream Of You/Everybody But Me.

Tilt: (UK) *Fontana 526 859-2 CD* (1995) (USA) *Drag City DC134CD* (1997)
Farmer In The City/The Cockfighter/Bouncer See Bouncer.../Manhattan/Face On Breast/Bolivia '95/Patriot (A Single)/Tilt/Rosary.

Til The Band Comes In: (UK) *Beat Goes On Records BGO CD 320* (1996) [reissue]
Prologue/Little Things (That Keep Us Together)/Joe/Thanks For Chicago Mr James/Long About Now/Time Operator/Jean The Machine/Cowbells Shakin'/Til The Band Comes In/The War Is Over/Stormy/The Hills Of Yesterday/Reuben James/What Are You Doing The Rest Of Your Life/It's Over.

It's Raining Today: The Scott Walker Story (1967–70): (USA) *Razor And Tie RE 2120-2* (1996):
Big Louise/Jackie/The World's Strongest Man/It's Raining Today/Montague Terrace (In Blue)/Through A Long And Sleepless Night/Next/The Seventh Seal/Plastic Palace People/Rosemary/The Old Man's Back Again/Joe/Lights Of Cincinnati/Cowbells Shakin'/Thanks For Chicago Mr James/Little Things (That Keep Us Together)/Joanna.

Looking Back With Scott Walker: (Germany) *Repertoire Records REP 4604-WY* (1996) [Tracks as per original Ember label release plus bonus tracks: Steady As A Rock/When Is A Boy A Man/The Livin' End/Good For Nothin'/Charley Bop/Golden Rule Of Love/Kathalene/I Broke My Own Heart/What Do You Say/Are These Really Mine/Crazy In Love With You/Forevermore/Anything Will Do]

To Have And To Hold: (Australia) *Mute Records IONIC15CD* (1996):
[Film soundtrack containing one vocal track by Scott: I Threw It All Away (Dylan). Remainder of CD features an original score by Nick Cave, Blixa Bargeld and Mick Harvey]

Stretch/We Had It All: (UK) *Beat Goes On Records BGO CD 358* (1997) [reissues: two albums on one CD]
Sunshine/Just One Smile/A Woman Left Lonely/No Easy Way Down/That's How I Got To Memphis/Use Me/Frisco Depot/Someone Who Cared/Where Does Brown Begin/Where Love Has Died/I'll Be Home/Low Down Freedom/We Had It All/Black Rose/Ride Me Down Easy/You're Young And You'll Forget/The House Song/Whatever Happened To Saturday Night/Sundown/Old Five And Dimers Like Me/Delta Dawn.

The Early Ten Years: (France) *Spalax 14566* (1997) [reissue, tracks as per the original Ember label release *Looking Back With Scott Walker*]

Looking Back With Scott Walker: (UK) *Ember EMB CD 3393* (TKO Music/Magnum Limited) (1998) [reissue, tracks as per the original Ember label release]

```
*******************************************************************

    The long-established, world-wide Appreciation
    Society for SCOTT WALKER is:




                    WALKERPEOPLE
                    C/o 71 Cheyne Court
                    Glengall Road
                    Woodford Green
                    Essex, IG8 ODN
                    ENGLAND




    Please include SAE/IRC with enquiries.

*******************************************************************
```

Creation Books International: http://www.pussycat.demon.co.uk
UK office/mail order sales:
83, Clerkenwell Road, London EC1R 5AR
Tel: 0171-430-9878 Fax: 0171-242-5527
E-mail: creation@pussycat.demon.co.uk
US office/mail order sales:
PO Box 13512, Berkeley, CA 94712 Tel: 510-540-7937
Creation products should be available in all proper bookstores; please ask your local retailer to order from:
UK & Europe: Turnaround Distribution, Unit 3 Olympia Trading Estate, Coburg Road, Wood Green, London N22 6TZ.
Tel: 0181-829-3000 Fax: 0181-881-5088
Benelux: Fringecore, Meibloemstraat 30, 2600 Berchem, Belgium
Tel: 03-239-6770 Fax: 03-281-3389 E-mail: dee@fringecore.com
Italy: Apeiron Editoria & Distribuzione, Piazza Orazio Moroni 4, 00060 Sant'Oresta (Roma). Tel: 0761-579670 Fax: 0761-579737
USA: Subterranean Company, Box 160, 265 South 5th Street, Monroe, OR 97456. Tel: 541-847-5274 Fax: 541-847-6018
US Non-Book Trade: Last Gasp, 777 Florida Street, San Francisco, CA 94110-0682. Tel: 415-824-6636 Fax: 415-824-1836
Canada: Marginal, Unit 102, 277 George Street, N. Peterborough, Ontario K9J 3G9. Tel/Fax: 705-745-2326
Australia & NZ: Peribo Pty Ltd, 58 Beaumont Road, Mount Kuring-gai, NSW 2080. Tel: 02-457-0011 Fax: 02-457-0022
Japan: Tuttle-Shokai, 21-13 Seki 1-Chome, Tama-ku, Kawasaki, Kanagawa 214. Tel: 44-833-1924 Fax: 44-833-7559

Other Jeremy Reed books from Creation:
The Last Star: A Study Of Marc Almond ISBN 1 871592 61 5
The Pleasure Chateau the classic of decadent erotica;
        ISBN 1 871592 52 6
Sister Midnight sequel to the Pleasure Chateau; ISBN 1 871592 80 1
Isidore a novelised life of le Comte de Lautréamont; ISBN 1 871592 42 9
Kicks an anthology of androgynous visions; ISBN 1 871592 15 1

Other music-related titles:
Destroy: Sex Pistols 1977 the photograph collection by Dennis Morris;
        ISBN 1 871592 74 7
Paradoxia: A Predator's Diary the confessions of Lydia Lunch;
        ISBN 1 871592 49 6